# Emotional Intelligence Mastery

The 2.0 Practical Guide to Boost Your EQ, Atomic Effective Techniques to Improve Your Social Skills, Self-Awareness, Relationships, and Making Friends – Why EQ Beats IQ

## Stephen Patterson

© Copyright 2019 - All rights reserved.

The content contained within this book may not be reproduced, duplicated or transmitted without direct written permission from the author or the publisher.

Under no circumstances will any blame or legal responsibility be held against the publisher, or author, for any damages, reparation, or monetary loss due to the information contained within this book. Either directly or indirectly.

**Legal Notice:**
This book is copyright protected. This book is only for personal use. You cannot amend, distribute, sell, use, quote or paraphrase any part, or the content within this book, without the consent of the author or publisher.

**Disclaimer Notice:**

Please note the information contained within this document is for educational and entertainment purposes only. All effort has been executed to present accurate, up to date, and reliable, complete information. No warranties of any kind are declared or implied. Readers acknowledge that the author is not engaging in the rendering of legal, financial, medical or professional advice. The content within this book has been derived from various sources. Please consult a licensed professional before attempting any techniques outlined in this book.

By reading this document, the reader agrees that under no circumstances is the author responsible for any losses, direct or indirect, which are incurred as a result of the use of information contained within this document, including, but not limited to, — errors, omissions, or inaccuracies.

# Contents

Introduction _____ 1

Chapter 1:
What Is Emotional Intelligence _____ 3

Chapter 2:
The Positive Effects of Emotional Intelligence _____ 15

Chapter 3:
Developing Emotional Intelligence _____ 21

Chapter 4:
Barriers to Emotional Intelligence _____ 37

Chapter 5:
EQ Trick #1: Reading Body Language _____ 53

Chapter 6:
EQ Trick #2: Releasing Destructive Emotions _____ 65

Chapter 7:
EQ Trick #3: Develop Social-Awareness _____ 73

Chapter 8:
EQ Trick #4: Building Empathy _____ 81

Chapter 9:
EQ Trick #5: Handing Conflicts the Right Way _____ 89

Chapter 10:
EQ Trick #6: Asking Critical Questions _____ 95

Chapter 11:
EQ Trick #7: Forgiving Your Past _____ 105

Chapter 12:
EQ Trick #8: Learn to Forgive _____ 111

Chapter 13:
EQ Trick #9: Make Others Feel Good Around You _____ 123

Chapter 14:
EQ Trick #10: Manage Anger _____ 129

Chapter 15:
FAQ _____ 135

Conclusion _____ 141

# EMOTIONAL INTELLIGENCE MASTERY

THE 2.0 PRACTICAL GUIDE TO BOOST
YOUR EQ, ATOMIC EFFECTIVE TECHNIQUES TO IMPROVE
YOUR SOCIAL SKILLS, SELF-AWARENESS, RELATIONSHIPS,
AND MAKING FRIENDS – WHY EQ BEATS IQ

## STEPHEN PATTERSON

Stephen Patterson

## Introduction

As crazy as it may seem, the brain uses the most energy. The brain switches through several emotions throughout a single day. There isn't a set limit on the number of emotions that person could experience. A person can wake up in the morning feeling fantastic, and by the time night rolls around, they feel depressed, angry, or sad.

Worries and preoccupations will often present their self in a person's mind. Certain events or moments can trigger different emotions. Everybody is their own person, but the brain is what can quickly change a person's life. It's essential that a person understands the way their mind works if they plan on feeling stronger about who they are.

It's incredible to look at the number of emotions that a person can experience during the day. The problem comes when those emotions cloud a person's judgment. People who can't handle those emotions will find it hard to think clearly.

Too many emotions at one time can end up causing mental fatigue. There are also times when a person will try to read how another person feels, but they aren't able to. They could end up misinterpreting their feelings and create an awkward moment.

It's crucial that a person can understand their emotions while also knowing how to manage them in the best way they can. The challenges that come up when a person tries to control their emotions will often cause frustration. It can also help a person to know how they can improve their emotions to help them out in crucial situations.

People who have high EQ are able to understand the needs of others. When you can work with a good EQ, it will be easier for a person to succeed. The best thing is, even if your EQ isn't the best right now, it can be developed with some time.

Stephen Patterson

# Chapter 1:
# What Is Emotional Intelligence

Emotional Intelligence, also known as EQ or EI is the capacity to handle with skill or control and identify your own emotions and the emotions of others. While psychologists often disagree about what real emotional intelligence is, it is typically believed to include at least three skill sets: the ability to manage emotions, which provides for regulating your own when needed and calming down or cheering up others; the ability to harness your feelings and use them for tasks such as problem-solving and thinking; and emotional awareness, or having the ability to name and identify your own emotions.

There isn't a valid scale or test for emotional intelligence like there is for general intelligence. This is why some critics like to claim that the concept of EQ is sketchy or doesn't exist. Despite the criticism, emotional intelligence has a large audience in the general public, and in specific industries. Over the last few years, some employers have started to incorporate "emotional intelligence tests" as part of the interview process or application. They believe that somebody that has a high emotional intelligence would make a better coworker or leader.

There have been a few studies which have found a link between job performance and emotional intelligence, but others haven't been able to find a correlation. With the lack of a scientifically valid scale creates a difficulty in being able to truly measure or predict a person's EQ on the job. A person who is emotionally intelligent is highly conscious of their own emotions, even if it's negative, and they can manage and identify them. These emotionally intelligent people are tuned in to the emotions that other people experience. It's easy to understand how being sensitive to emotions from within and in the environment around you can make a person a better romantic partner, leader, parent, or friend. Fortunately for everybody, these skills can be improved.

The term emotional intelligence made its first appearance in a 1964 paper written by Michael Baloch. It appeared again in a 1966 article by B. Leaner titled Emotional Intelligence and Emancipation, which was published in the Practice of Child Psychology and Child Psychiatry journal. Howard Gardner introduced the idea that traditional intelligence, like IQ, doesn't fully explain a person's cognitive ability in his 1983 book Frames of Mind: The Theory of Multiple Intelligences. In the book, he introduced the belief of multiple intelligences, which includes intrapersonal intelligence and interpersonal intelligence.

While emotional intelligence appeared in many texts throughout the years, it didn't become widely known until Daniel Goleman's 1995 book, Emotional Intelligence – Why It Can Matter More Than IQ. Due to the book's best-selling status, the term became popular. Emotional intelligence also refers to a person's ability to join emotions, intelligence, and empathy to improve understanding and thought of interpersonal dynamics. Different models of EQ have led to the creation of various instruments for assessment. While many of the measures do overlap, the majority of researchers agree that they focus on different constructs.

For a lot of people, their Emotional Quotient has a lot of relevance and significant value as compared to Intelligence Quotient in achieving their aspirations and goals in life, which we will talk about later in this chapter. As individuals, all of our success depends on the aptitude in understanding signals around him/her which, in turn, you will act upon appropriately. Therefore, everybody needs to develop ripe EI skills that are necessary for perceiving, negotiating, and empathizing with others. Otherwise, success will stay just out of our grasp.

## Five Categories

Howard Gardner, an influential Harvard theorist said, "Your EQ is the level of your ability to understand other people, what motivates them, and how to work cooperatively with them." There are five main categories of emotional intelligence skills that researchers currently recognize. In order to improve your EQ, it's important to understand these five areas.

## 1. Self-Awareness

This is the capacity in recognizing one's internal state of being and the involuntary physiological response to an object or a situation, based on or tied to physical state and sensory data. This is a crucial step in your emotional intelligence. To promote the growth of this, it will require that you check what you are really feeling. Hence, in assessing your emotions, you'll be able to manage it as a result. The two principles of great significance in self-awareness are:

- Emotional awareness: This refers to the aptitude in recognizing your internal state of being and the way it impacts you.

- Self-confidence: This is the sureness you have about your capabilities and self-worth.

## 2. Self-Regulation

The unfortunate thing about emotions is that you don't have all that much control over when you experience them. You can, however, have a little bit of say in the amount of time the emotion lasts through the use of some techniques in ameliorating undesirable internal state of being like depression, anxiety, and anger. Some of the techniques contain actions such as casting something into a different form, seeing a specific moment under a better point of view, or aspect from which a concept, person or thing is regarded; go on a hiking or be in motion like walking around the block or in nature/park; and meditating or praying. Self-regulation will often involve:

- Innovation: This means being open to new things.

- Adaptability: This means you can handle change with flexibility.

- Conscientiousness: This means you take responsibility for your performance.

- Trustworthiness: This means that you maintain standards of integrity and honesty.

- Self-control: This means you can manage disruptive impulses.

## 3. Motivation

In order to encourage oneself to achieve something, it will require goals free of ambiguity or doubt and attitude on the brighter side of the spectrum. While a person might be inclined either in the negative or positive attitudes, you are able to, with practice and effort, think more positively. If you are able to catch a negative thought when it occurs, you will then be able to reconstruct it into its better side and as a result, this will aid you to obtain your aspirations in life. This category of EI consists of the following four things:

- Optimism: You continue to pursue goals even though you have setbacks and hit obstacles.

- Initiative: You get ready to act on opportunities.

- Commitment: You align yourself with the goals of the organization or group.

Achievement drive: You constantly strive to further or promote a personal growth in order to satisfy and comply a certain level or ideal, size, amount, power, quality, etc.

## 4. Empathy
This is the ability to recognize how another person feels, and this is crucial in achieving a successful career and life. If you are good at

comprehending the hidden feelings of a person's outward signs, you will be able to have a good management of your personal signs that they may see on you. Oftentimes, people with empathy excel in:

- Understanding others: Being able to discern the feelings behind what others want and need.

- Political awareness: Being able to read a group's power relationships and emotional currents.

- Leveraging diversity: Being able to create opportunities through diverse people.

- Developing others: Being able to sense what other people need to bolster, progress, and their abilities.

- Service orientation: Recognizing, meeting, and anticipating a client's needs.

## 5. Social Skills

Creating good interpersonal skills is tantamount to having success in your career and life. In our ever-connected world, everybody has instant access to technical knowledge. This makes people skills even more important now than ever before because you need to have a high

EQ in order to understand, negotiate, and empathize with other people in a global economy. The most useful skills include:

- Team capabilities: Being about to create group synergy in pursuing a collective goal.

- Cooperation and collaboration: You work with others toward a shared goal.

- Building bonds: Being able to nurture important relationships.

- Conflict management: Being able to resolve, understand, and negotiate disagreements.

- Change catalyst: Knowing how to manage or initiate change.

- Leadership: Knowing how to guide and inspire people and groups.

- Communication: Being able to send clear messages.

- Influence: Being able to use effective persuasion tactics.

Why is it that there are people that have high IQs who miss attaining their desired goals while the others with modest IQs are able to do so? Both IQ and EQ can be used in determining how you will fare in your career and life. However, intelligence quotient is insufficient on its own.

Emotional quotient plays an important role as well that even the experts in the field of psychology concur that intelligence quotient only accounts 10% or 25% at best amidst the important things needed in attaining your aspirations. All of the rest is dependent on everything else, and this includes EQ.

One study performed on graduates at Harvard medicine, business, law, and teaching found zero or negative correlation between an IQ indicator and their subsequence success in their careers. Let's dive a little deeper into the importance of EQ and IQ.

## EQ Over IQ

So, what really is more important in determining life success: street smarts or book smarts? This is what really gets to the heart of a debate contrasting the related importance of IQ and EQ.

People who prefer book smarts will likely suggest that our IQ will play the biggest role in determining how successful we will be in life. People who prefer street smarts will likely suggest that a person's EQ is more important. So, which one is it?

In Daniel Goleman's 1996 book, Emotional Intelligence, he suggested that EQ may be more important than IQ. The reason for this is because some psychologists believe that standard intelligence measures tend to be too narrow and don't take into account the full range of human intelligence. Howard Gardner, a psychologist, suggested that intelligence isn't a single ability. Instead, he believes that people have multiple intelligences and that people can have strengths in many different areas.

Instead of looking at a single, general intelligence, which is typically referred to as the 'g factor', there are some people who believe that the ability to express and understand emotions can play an equal, possibly more, important role in how well a person will do in life. You understand what EQ is, but let's look at what exactly IQ refers to. IQ, or intelligence quotient, is a number figured out through a standardized intelligence test. The original IQ tests calculated their scores by dividing the person's mental age by their actual age and then multiplied it by 100. This means that a child who had a mental age of 15 and was 10 years old would have an IQ score of 150. Now they score IQ tests by comparing the results to scores of other people in their age group.

- IQ shows abilities like:

- *Quantitative reasoning*

- *Short-term and working memory*

- *Fluid reasoning*

- *Knowledge of the world*

- *Spatial and visual processing*

Now that we know what IQ and EQ are, which one is more important? At one time, IQ was seen as the main way to figure out a person's success. They assumed that those who had high IQs were destined for a life of achievement and accomplishment and the researchers debated as to whether or not intelligence was the product of the environment or genes. However, critics started to notice that not only was a high IQ no guarantee for life success, it was also too narrow of a concept to completely encompass the range of human knowledge and abilities. IQ is still seen as an important part of success, especially for academic success. People who have a high IQ will typically do well in school, earn more money, and are healthier in general. Now experts recognize it's not the only determining factor of life success. Instead, it's a single part of a very complex array of influences that encompasses EQ among other things.

Emotional intelligence has had a very big impact in a number of areas, which include the business world. A lot of companies mandate EQ training and makes EQ tests a part of their hiring process. There is one insurance company that found that EQ could play a large role in sales success. Sales agents who had lower EQ abilities like self-confidence, empathy, and initiative were found to sell policies that had an average premium of $54,000. The agents whose EQ was higher sold policies with a premium of $114,000.

Emotional abilities are also able to influence the choices that shoppers make when they are faced with a decision. Daniel Kahneman was able to discover that people like to deal with others that they trust instead of somebody they don't, even if they have to pay more for a product that is inferior.

Success in life is due to many different factors. Both EQ and IQ play important roles in influencing a person's success, as well as things like happiness, health, and wellness. It's important that you work to strengthen all of your skills. Work to improve your emotional and social skills, as well as your mental focus and memory.

## Chapter 2:
## The Positive Effects of Emotional Intelligence

We all know that the smartest people in the world aren't necessarily the most successful or most fulfilled. You likely know people who were academically brilliant but were socially inept and they weren't successful at work or in relationships. As we learned in the last chapter, IQ isn't enough all by itself to be successful. Yes, a person's IQ can help them get accepted into college, but it's your EQ that is going to help you manage the emotions and stress that you will face during final exams. EQ and IQ exist in tandem and work the best when they build off of each other.

### The Importance of Positive Emotions

Over a long period of time, psychologists had been focused on studying the undesirable emotions and its effects which include: anxiety, stress, anger, sadness, and depression. Psychologists flock towards these because they often indicate that there is a disorder.

In spite of that, positive emotions have interesting qualities and are also captivating. People often think that the positive effect disrupts or distorts orderly and efficient consideration or assessment of things or events around him/her and this is why positive emotions were deemed "simple." Since it tends to exist for only a short period of time, it couldn't possibly influence or affect someone over a relatively long time period.

Studies found out that this just isn't the case, but it took them a while to reach that conclusion. Only recently have psychologists realized that positive emotions are important in itself, hence, they set into motion of studying it. Barbara Fredrickson is the one responsible in this realization. She devoted much time to her studies on this topic since she wanted to find out the advantages of having these positive emotions.

It's clear to see what negative emotions can do. Fear chips in into the inclination of fleeing or getting away from something or someone. Anger will often cause an attack. If our ancestors didn't have these, our beinghood would have been uncertain. In addition to what has been said, these types of internal state of being will restrict the human's reactions to situations such as running when we are in danger.

Negative emotions are also able to minimize distractions in acute situations. Positive emotions aren't connected with certain actions, so why are they important, apart from making use feel good? Why do we need to feel happy, ecstatic, affectionate, or joyful?

## Where Emotional Intelligence Affects Your Life

### How You Perform at Work or School?

Having a high emotional intelligence will be able to help you navigate all of the social complexities in the workplace, motivate and lead others, and excel at your work. As you know, there are a lot of companies that now look at EQ.

### How Physically Healthy You Are?

If you find it hard to manage your emotions, then you will likely find it hard to manage your stress. This can end up causing serious health problems. When stress remains uncontrolled, it can increase your blood pressure, increase your risk of stroke and heart attack, suppress your immune system, cause infertility, and speed up the aging process. The first thing you need to do to improve your emotional intelligence is to figure out how to manage your stress.

### How Mentally Healthy You Are?

Uncontrolled stress and emotions will also have a large impact on your mental health, which makes you vulnerable to depression and anxiety. If you find it is hard to understand, manage, or be comfortable with your emotions, you will also end up struggling to create strong relationships. This can end up causing you to feel isolated and lonely and will further worsen mental health issues.

### If You Can Create Healthy Relationships?

When you grasp your own internal state of being and find ways of managing it the best, you will be better at expressing how you feel and better understand how other people feel. This will give you the ability to communicate in a more effective manner and create stronger relationships, both in your personal life and at work.

### How Socially Intelligent You Are?

When you are in tune with your emotions it will serve a social purpose and will connect you with other people and the world. Social intelligence is what will enable you to recognize a friend from a foe, measure how much another person is interested in you, lower stress and balance out the nervous system through communication and feel happy and loved.

## You Will Be Able to Make Better Decisions?

If you are able to understand yourself and the people around you, and you can control your behavior, thoughts, and feelings, as well as the behavior of others, you will be able to make goals that are consistent with who you really are and that don't harm the relationships you have. You will also be able to make decisions that aren't created through distortions, emotional reactions, and assumptions.

You can give others the things that they actually want? Understanding another person's feelings and thoughts will allow you to anticipate the things that make them happy and empower you to provide them with the things that they want. Improved empathy and understanding will help you to put yourself into their lives and understand the needs of the people around you. When you are able to understand others and communicate the understanding, the people around you will be more likely to be happy when in a relationship with you.

# Emotional Intelligence Mastery

## Chapter 3:
## Developing Emotional Intelligence

As you now understand that EQ can help you understand yourself and increase your odds of achieving your goals, you probably want to know if there is a way to improve your emotional intelligence. Peter Salovey and David R. Caruso, professors of The Emotionally Intelligent Manager, broke down the core skills that are involved when it comes to increasing emotional intelligence:

- Figuring out your own feelings and the feelings of others.

- Using feelings to help guide your reasoning and thinking, along with others.

- Understanding the fact that feelings may change and develop as things happen.

- Being about to remain open to the data of feelings and use this for actions and decisions.

While you will find ten tricks later in this book that will help you to increase your emotional intelligence, there are some steps we are going to look at how to help you get started.

## Think or Ponder Seriously on Your Internal State of Being.

Sit back and relax, give yourself time in considering and thinking of ways on how to utilize your feelings. For instance, consider what your normal responses are to these situations:

- An associate or close friend starts to unexpectedly cry.

- Another driver cuts you off.

- Your romantic partner blames you for something that you think is unfair.

- You receive an email that implies that you messed something up.

By figuring out your own reactions and emotions, you will be more mindful; hence you can set into motion the steps in creating restraint and safeguard or find countermeasures. It also helps to look at how you respond at the moment. Do you tend to rush to judgment before you take the time to learn all of the facts? Do you often use stereotypes? Take an honest look at how you interact with others and think. Try putting yourself in their position and try to become more accepting and open of their needs and perspectives.

Another area to take a look at is stressful situations. How do you react when things become stressful? Do you often become very upset when there is a delay or if something doesn't go the way you want? Do you often blame other people or become angry at others, even when they had nothing to do with it? Having the ability to remain calm and in control in stressful situations is an amazing skill. It's important to keep your emotions under control when things don't go exactly as planned.

**Ask Other People for Their Point of View.**
We are often unaware of how others see us and usually, this is distinct or not the same way in how we view ourselves, and the same applies conversely. This has nothing to do with being right or wrong. All that is important is understanding the way perceptions differ, and the consequences that it creates.

When we ask those that are close to us, such as a close friend, coworker, or a significant other, about how we interact with them, we will learn something from their perspective. You can ask them regarding that moment wherein you are extremely emotional. Enquire them if you acted differently from the usual and if they can portray that. You can also enquire on the similar experiences that they have gone through when they were very emotional. A couple of other questions you could ask are:

- Would you describe me as sensitive to your emotions and feelings?

- In what way had I treated you at that particular moment?

Finding out the responses or replies to the said enquiries will assist you in making yourself see the way other people view you thereby making you understand other people better as well. This knowledge can then be used to adjust how you deal with others.

## Be More Observant.

Armed with your new-found knowledge, you are now able to be more observant of your emotions. Your own self-reflection, as well as what others have told you, can help you to tune into what you are feeling. If you do make new discoveries, repeat the first step. If you want, you can write down your experience. Doing this will help you to clarify your thinking so that you stay in "learning mode."

In your observations, take a look at your work environment. Do you tend to seek attention for the things you accomplish? Humility is a quality that a lot of people lack, and it doesn't mean that you lack confidence or are shy. When you have humility, you are letting people know that you know what you accomplished, and you quietly are confident about it. Allow those around you to shine. Place some focus on them, and don't focus so much on getting your own praise.

## Make Sure That You Use "The Pause."

Make sure that you utilize "the pause." "The pause" is simply spending a few minutes to desist your responses and ponder on it prior to speaking or acting on it. Supposing that everybody tried this, imagine how much shorter an email would be, the amount of time that would be saved during meetings, and the number of inflammatory or emotionally charged written or spoken remarks in social media that we could do away with.

It is important to remember that "the pause" might be simple theoretically. On the other hand, practicing it is hard and requires much effort. Although you might be good at handling your emotions in general, factors such as a bad day or added stress could affect your ability to do so at a specific time. I'm not just talking about upsetting situations. People tend to propel oneself headfirst at occasions or circumstances they think are amazing in that particular moment which, unfortunately, they actually didn't fully consider and understand all the consequences associated with it. In making sure that you take the time to pause before you act or speak, you will create a habit of thinking first instead of acting first.

### Take Some Time to Delve into The Causes, Reasons, Or Purposes.

Majority of people will concur that compassion and empathy are crucial parts of a beneficial and healthy relationship. Why is it that we tend to neglect to show those qualities when it's most important, such as when we don't show understanding to a close partner or friend when they experience a tough time?

Scientists have looked at what Adam Grant, a psychologist, calls, "the perspective gap." In short, this refers to the fact that it is extremely hard to put ourselves in somebody else's shoes. We tend to forget how certain situations feel, even if we have gone through a similar situation. Supposedly that you haven't experienced the same situation, envision how limited our points of view will be because of that.

### In What Way Will This Gap Be Closed?

Attributes such as compassion and empathy will aid us in trying to put ourselves in another person's shoes. On the other hand, it is important that we take extra steps instead of just being satisfied in utilizing the self-experiences only. To show a legit and sincere/pure empathy, it is necessary that all "whys" are explored.

- Why do I feel differently than they do?

- Why are they dealing with that I can't see?

- Why do they feel the way they do?

If you aren't able to effectively answer those questions, think about working with the person for some time to really understand what they are going through, as seen from their perspective. Doing this will help you to view your family members and team, not as complainers, but for who they really are: people who need help.

Every time a person criticizes you, try not to be offended. Instead, enquire yourself on what things, lessons, or knowledge this particular event will impact on you.

No matter if you are a loyal employee or a successful entrepreneur, criticism isn't easy to take. You have poured blood, sweat, and tears into your work. It can be hard when a person comes in and destroys what you have created.

The truth is, criticism tends to be rooted in truth, even if it's not delivered in the best way. When you end up getting negative feedback, you have two choices: You can place your feelings to the side and try to learn from what happened, or you can get angry and allow your emotions to get the best of you. When a critical judgment is passed or expressed on us, regardless of how well it was done or not, what is important is that you take time and think or ponder on it. Give these a thought:

- Set aside your personal feelings and ask yourself the possible things that you could learn if you look at things through their vantage point.

- Instead of focusing on how they delivered their message, how can I make use of their feedback to help me or my team do better?

There may be times, though, that you don't need to listen to the criticism. For example, if the criticism is based on falsehood or if it is given in a way that was meant to destroy your self-worth. Typically, that isn't the case. To improve ourselves, we shouldn't let ourselves be clouded by our emotions so much that we can't properly give an assessment to a negative feedback thrown our way. In lieu of this, let us allow ourselves an attempt to gain knowledge so as to improve.

## Keep on Practicing.

Just like with every other skill or ability, practicing will make it better. Of course, it will be impossible to perfectly control your emotions. Learning how you can improve your emotional intelligence isn't a process that will happen overnight. However, if you consistently practice these steps, and the tricks you will learn later in the book, will allow you to harness the power of emotions. You will then be able to utilize the said power instead of it in opposition to yourself.

## Sex Differences

Currently, research has found that women tend to have higher emotional intelligence. This is based on common ability tests like the Test of Emotional Intelligence and MSCEIT. Studies of physiological measures, reviews, meta-analysis, brain neuroimaging, and behavioral tests support these findings.

The MSCEIT, or the Mayer Salovey Caruso Emotional Intelligence Test, is a test that scores a person's emotional intelligence. A study published in *Personality and Individual Differences* in 2004, looked at a 246-university sample and found that women scored higher than men on every scale of the MSCEIT. Another study that was published that same year, and in that same journal, looked at 330 people and also found that women scored higher in emotional intelligence.

A study published in *Sex Roles* in 2011 looked at the findings of Dasher Keltner and Matthew J. Hartenstein. They found that in their behavioral experiment of 212 participants, women experienced more emotions, communicated more happiness, and felt more pro-social emotions in a one on one dyadic interaction. They also found that 79% of the females could accurately decode male emotions, and 96% accurately decoded female emotions. For males, 70% were able to correctly identify male emotions and 81% could correctly identify female emotions.

A 2014 analysis published in *Neuroscience & Biobehavioral Reviews* found that sex differences in empathy could be seen from birth, and they would grow larger with age and would remain stable and consistent throughout their lifespan. Females have higher empathy than men at every age stage. Children who had higher levels of empathy, regardless of their gender, continue to possess high empathy during their life.

Further analysis using brain tools found females who watched a human suffer had higher ERP waves than men did. This is an indication of a better empathic response. A different investigation that used similar tools, like an N400 amplitude, discovered women had higher N400 in response to social situations, which correlated with their empathy.

Studies that used structural fMRIs also discovered that women had a larger grey matter in their anterior inferior parietal and posterior inferior frontal cortex areas. Throughout history, women nurtured and were the main caretakers of the children, so this has probably led to an advanced neurological adaptation for them so that they could be more aware and responsive to non-verbal cues. Prehistoric men didn't have to face the same selective pressure, so this could explain the modern-day differences in empathy and emotion recognition.

## Childhood

Not only does emotional intelligence vary by genders, but your childhood could also affect your emotional intelligence. Children learn what they see, so children raised by parents who had low emotional intelligence will likely struggle.

Let's take this as an example. A ten-year-old girl lies in bed, happy that she is behind the closed doors of her bedroom. "It's possible," she whispered to herself. In her mind she is going through the fantasy that she has used to help her through her life: her father answers the knock on the door and a well-dressed couple explains that his daughter was accidentally sent home with the wrong family and that they are her real parents. They take her back with them, where they love and nurture her.

The young girl doesn't realize it, but this is only the start of her struggle. She is going to spend the following 20 years wishing that her parents were different, and she will feel guilty about it. Her parents are basically good. They work and make sure that their daughter has toys, clothes, food, and a roof over her head. She goes to school and does her homework every day. She plays soccer and has a few friends. From the outside, she is a lucky child.

Despite her "luck," and even though she is loved by her parents, at the age of 10 she feels that, deep down, she is alone. How is a 10-year-old able to know this? Why does she feel like this? There is no simple answer. Her parents have low emotional intelligence. She is struggling with Childhood Emotional Neglect. When you have parents that lack emotional skills and awareness, you will struggle for several good reasons:

- When your parents don't know their own emotions, they aren't able to speak the language of emotion in your home.

Instead of saying something like, "You look down sweetheart. Did something happen at school?" All your parents would likely say is, "So how was school?" When your grandparent passes away, your family walks through the funeral as if it's no big deal. If you were stood up by your prom date, your family supports you by not talking about it, or they tease you about it, and they never notice or even care how you feel. This will result in you not learning how to be self-aware. You don't ever realize that your feelings are important or real. You won't ever learn how to talk about, sit with, or feel your emotions.

- Since your parents aren't all that good at controlling and managing their emotions, they won't be able to teach you the best way to control and manage your emotions.

If you were to get in trouble at school for calling your teacher a name, your parents won't ask what was going on or why you got upset. They won't explain to you how you could have better handled the problem. Instead, you will be grounded, or they yell or they will blame the teacher and let you off the hook. This will result in you not learning how to manage or control your feelings or how to take care of difficult situations.

- Since your parents aren't able to understand emotions, they will end up sending you the wrong message about yourself and the world through how they act and what they say.

Your parents will often act as if you're lazy because they haven't been able to pick up on the anxiety that is holding you back from doing things. Your siblings may treat you as if you're weak or call you a crybaby because you cried for several days after your pet was hit by a car. This will cause you to go forward into adulthood with negative voices in your head that call you lazy or weak. All of this will end up leaving you confused, struggling, and baffled. You will be out of touch with who you are. You view yourself through the eyes of different people who don't know you, and you will have a lot of difficulties handing difficult, stressful, or conflictual situations.

Fortunately, though, it's not too late for you or the little girl in our story. There are plenty of things that you can do. You and the little girl in our story can't continue to fantasize about a knock on the door. You have to face reality and learn emotional skills on your own since your parents didn't do a good job. You can reverse the effects of Childhood Emotional Neglect. Learning about emotions and learning who you really are can help you create a stepping stone. Also, while you may want to blame everything on your parents because that's an easy way out, it's better if you try to understand why they did what they did. Chances are, they were raised by parents who were emotional neglectful. Maybe, if you are able to improve your emotional intelligence, and you show them your new skills, they might just rub off on them.

# Chapter 4:
# Barriers to Emotional Intelligence

According to the philosopher and mathematician, Rene Descartes, "Everything is self-evident." Everything is self-evident if a person has high emotional intelligence and does well at testing reality. If your mind is constantly overloaded with emotions, stuck in the past, inauthentic, inflexible, or inept at non-verbal and verbal communication, everything won't be self-evident. When you are able to develop your emotional intelligence, and your ability to manage and understand your own emotions as well as those of the people around you, you will start to see things more clearly. You will be able to avoid these pitfalls to smart choices and accurate perception:

- How you wish things were.

- How you believe things should be.

- Believing that how things have been going in the past is how they are going to go now, and how they will always be.

- Assuming things about situations in-the-moment which appears on the surface to be close to people and experiences in the past. You always need to check out assumptions.

- Your persona or unintegrated, inauthentic self, which changes according to your situation, emotion, and mood without an anchor or a compass.

- Your ability to delude yourself because you lack knowledge about yourself.

- Self-sabotaging because you lack self-management, self-knowledge, and have a low EQ.

- Jealousy, anger, fear, and other types of strong emotions that distort your thinking.

- Hearing the things that you want to hear or need to hear instead of the things that are really being said. Failing to consider the other person's non-verbal clues.

- View distortion from relying too much on another person's perception of reality or catching their emotions.

We are our emotions. Emotions are what influence our perception of what's real. The more you are able to understand your emotions and yourself, the better you will be able to understand how your emotions affect your perceptions of what is around you and you will be able to manage them so that you are able to make smart choices.

Emotions are what guide us and provide us with information, but there are times when we have to get to the neocortex to make the best decision. For example, you could be feeling angry and you feel like hitting somebody, but your "thinking brain" will let you know this isn't a smart idea. By the same token, you could be in love with somebody, which is the limbic brain, while your neocortex provides you with a bunch of reasons not to love them.

The most important decisions will normally need to be made with the mind and the heart. Let's look at the three main reasons why people end up having trouble increasing their EQ.

## Avoiding the Truth

Knowledge is power, but for many people when it comes to self-knowledge, ignorance is bliss. Watch any sitcom, and you will likely notice that it takes advantage of a simple fact of human psychology that will make us all laugh. This set-up will normally look something like this:

The main character will tell their partner, "I wouldn't compromise my ethics for money." Later on, that same character will be offered an opportunity to compromise their ethics for money, and they say yes to it.

The funny part isn't only the hypocrisy but also the complete unawareness that the character has of their hypocrisy. When we watch this, we will probably assume it isn't intended to diagnose human psychology. Instead, it's a way of creating a joke at the expense of the character. In reality, it's a great example of how people will always avoid the truth about their self. In a paper published in the Review of General Psychology in 2010, they explained three main reasons people will avoid the truth about their self:

It could end up causing them to have to change their beliefs. There is a lot of evidence that suggests that people will often seek information that confirms what they believe instead of information that disproves them.

It could mean that we have to take undesired actions. Letting the doctor know about a weird symptom could mean that you have to undergo a painful test. There are times when it seems better to not know.

It could end up causing unpleasant emotions.

It's easy to see that all three motivations are in play with the sitcom example we used earlier. Weighed against it all, which motivates us to figure out the truth, are the reasons you would expect such as hope and curiosity for positive information. Whether or not we try to figure out the truth or stay away from it will depend on the following things:

Expectation: This is probably the most obvious and maybe the most powerful. The more often we expect bad news, the more effort we will take to try and avoid it.

Lack of Control: This is less obvious, but it does explain a lot of things. When we feel as if we don't have as much control over the consequences of information, we are often motivated to avoid it. For example, when you might get news about a life-threatening disease. Since there isn't much that you could do about it, it could be better to not find out.

Very Few Coping Resources: When people think that they aren't able to handle distressing information in a particular moment, then they will likely avoid it.

When the Information Is Difficult to Figure Out: The harder it is for a person to interpret the information, the less likely they will want to know it.

People tend to do their best to stay away from learning about themselves and this sometimes makes sense. For example, a genetic test could tell you that you are at a higher risk of atrial fibrillation after the age of 70. Would this be useful information, or would it just give you more things to worry about? If you can't do anything about it, then it is likely information that will decrease your quality of life.

Then there are times when we hurt ourselves by avoiding information. This can be seen when we refuse to have a mole checked and end up delaying cancer treatment. The tricky thing is knowing the information that you should avoid and which information you need to seek out. But we aren't able to do this without finding out the information. After you have learned the information, you are unable to unlearn it. This is the problem. Unfortunately, there is no clear solution. Now, you could find that you are asking, "Why do I need to care about not facing the truth?"

Not facing the truth, or self-deception comes with profound costs even if it is commonplace and normative. We all live our truth, whether we are completely honest with yourself. Self-deception is seen in our relationships, emotional reactions, behaviors, beliefs, and thinking patterns. Anytime our life ends up being driven by something out of our awareness, it becomes dangerous to people around us and our self.

## Stephen Patterson

The biggest cost of self-deception is that we will likely hurt ourselves and the people closest to use when we don't take complete responsibility for our self. One of the most common excuses people make for not being their ideal version is their painful life experiences. Anytime that happens, we will indirectly and directly hurt other people, especially people we love.

Another cost comes in when we cause large-scale acts of cruelty by believing the lies and spreading them to other people. While the majority of us say that we couldn't deliberately harm another, history and social psychology suggest that everybody is capable of extreme acts of cruelty if we are placed in the right environment. For example, if some people were able to convince you that they were going to kill you and everybody that you loved, would you allow them to perform their systematic extermination? History tells us that we would, but we are willing to deceive our self into believing that we couldn't.

The third cost of self-deception is that we could end up with a huge amount of regret. We have likely made choices that have harmful consequences in order to stay away from honesty. Or we might have decided to change once we admitted the truth. Having to look back at your life with regret is a tough thing to get over because you can't change the decisions you made in the past. The only choices that matter is the present one.

## Trying to Be Perfect

The desire to be perfect affects a lot of people and will doom them to a life of unhappiness. At first, you could think that aiming for perfection is desirable. We're going to take a deeper look at this belief. Perfection suggests that there is a state of flawlessness, without any type of defects. Aiming for perfection with a particular task could be done and there are some students who can strive to attain a perfect grade, or you could try to do a perfect job at something. Yet, having the goal of being perfect in life is extremely different.

An electronic device or a machine could operate perfectly, but only for a while. Over time it is going to wear down and needs some form of repair. The notion of perfection is deeply rooted in the paradigm of Newton's mechanistic universe. Humans have never been meant to be perfect. That's what it means to be human. Think about the saying "I'm only human." It's important that you remind yourself that your goal shouldn't be to emulate a machine, but you should embrace the imperfection of a human life.

## Stephen Patterson

Our culture has long been moving relentlessly towards an emphasis on goal orientation and achievement. When this happens, we lose the capacity of awe and wonder. Could you picture viewing a rainbow and then complaining that one of the colors didn't look perfect? Not only is that completely ridiculous, but we would also end up ruining the splendor at that moment. But that is exactly what we tend to do when we judge ourselves for things that we do imperfectly. We tend to forget that humans are a part of nature as well. We would benefit a lot if we started to accept the natural state of our life, which happens to be imperfect.

The pursuit of perfectionism tends to be a disguise for insecurity. Ironically, if a person actually achieved this state of impossible perfection, there's a good chance that very few people will be able to tolerate them. The perfect individual would be a constant reminder of the shortcomings in others.

Most people will strive for perfection because they are trying to compensate for a sense of inadequacy. They typically have an exaggerated view of their shortcomings. They probably heard messages earlier in their life that they weren't good enough. So, they figured that being perfect was the only option. Perfectionists often have this sense that other people are better than they are, so they have to be completely without flaws so that they can catch up. This is a very dangerous myth. The closest to perfection that you can get it making sure that you are fully present.

## The Fear of The Uncertain

Read any type of "Dear Abby" type column and you will start to notice a reoccurring theme. A lot of people will ask questions concerning big decisions. They want somebody else to help them make these decisions because they are afraid to make them their self. Why? They are afraid of the uncertain. Once they get an answer from their neutral third-party, they will be able to act, see what comes of it, and stop living in an anxious state of anticipation. More times than not, it's often the not-knowing that is the worst.

One of the biggest downsides of human consciousness is our ability to worry about our future. We know that the future exists, but we are unsure of what is going to happen. A postdoctoral research associate at the University of Wisconsin-Madison's Center of Investing Healthy Minds, Dan Gruppe, says that, "In other animals, unpredictability or uncertainty can lead to heightened vigilance, but I think what's unique about humans is the ability to reflect on the fact that these future events are unknown or unpredictable." The feelings of uncertainty can end up causing a bunch of distress, especially for humans.

As humans, we have the habit of choosing something with certitude over ones that are ambiguous. Studies found out that humans want to be shocked now as compared to getting the shock later. They also show a greater nervous-system activation when they have to wait for the shock or any other unpleasant stimulus. What is different among people is how much uncertainty will bother them.

The Intolerance of Uncertainty Scale was developed in 1994, and this scale figures out how much people want predictability, and how they will react in situations that are uncertain. A higher level of intolerance is known as "cognitive vulnerability." The researchers in Quebec who created the scale linked high IU to anxiety disorders, and, to a lesser degree, depression and eating disorders. Michel Dugas has done the majority of his research on generalize anxiety disorder, and he says that IU is a causal risk factor, meaning it doesn't have a strong link to GAD. Instead, higher IU has been found to lead to more worry.

**Self-Sabotage**
Self-sabotaging is any behavior that creates a problem in your life and interferes with your long-term goals. Some of the most common self-sabotaging behaviors are forms of self-injury, comfort eating, self-medication, and procrastination. At that moment, the acts could seem

helpful, but ultimately, they are going to undermine your success, especially if you engage in them repeatedly.

A lot of people won't even realize that they are self-sabotaging, or they won't realize the damage it is causing because the effects will likely take some time to show up. Unfortunately, being able to connect a behavior to self-sabotaging consequences isn't a guarantee that a person will stop doing the behavior. Still, there is a chance for the person to overcome nearly all forms of self-sabotage. Behavioral therapies can help in interrupting ingrained thought actions and patterns while also strengthening self-regulation and deliberation. Motivational therapies are able to connect people with their values and goals. One novel form of self-sabotage interventions are computer programs that will eliminate the constant temptation of distractions that happen online.

Our self-sabotaging habits come from a critical inner voice. This voice is created from our early life experiences. Without knowing it, we will often internalize attitudes that influential caretakers or parents directed toward us during our development. For example, if your parents viewed you as lazy, you will likely grow up feeling ineffective or useless. This may cause you to engage in self-sabotaging thoughts or acts that tell you not to even try, such as, what's the point, you won't succeed anyway?

Children are also able to internalize negative thoughts that their caretakers or parents had toward themselves. If you grew up with parents who hated their self, who viewed their self as a failure or weak, you may end up growing up with some of the similar self-sabotaging attitudes toward yourself. For example, if your parent was always critical about the way they looked, you may end up experiencing some of the same insecurities without knowing it. You would likely feel easily self-conscious and less sure of yourself in public or social situations.

The way your self-sabotage can come out in several different ways and will manifest in your life in several ways. The following is a list of typical methods that you often use to get in your own way when it comes to success.

- You allow yourself to succumb to a fear of failure.

- You don't allow yourself to take risks.

- You don't take proactive action because you are afraid to make mistakes.

- You decide to ignore important instructions.

- Taking time in making plans is not your thing.

- You find it hard to tell another people no.

- You do not ponder on the possible effects your actions might have on others.

- You make decisions without thinking it thoroughly.

- You don't make an effort to critically or practically think about our circumstances.

- You are too set in your ways and you refuse to think flexibly about your problems.

- You have too much pride to admit when you make a mistake or an error.

- You constantly worry without taking a look at your situation objectively.

- You create unrealistic expectations for yourself and others.

- You let your critical voice take charge and you start to persistently judge yourself and others.

- You continuously indulge in comparison thinking where you measure your values based on the things that others do.

- You always complain about circumstances, life, and people, or perceived bad luck.

- You knowingly indulge in perfectionism and procrastination.

- You blindly accept the advice of others without questioning it.

- You struggle with poor attitudes, debilitating emotions, and limiting beliefs.

- You persistently indulge in thoughts that are unhelpful and sabotage your mind.

- You regularly focus on the things that don't work or on wishful daydreams.

It is of significant value that you do not ignore the limiting thoughts you have including the excuses that you tend to make that keep you from moving forward. Every pattern listed will come with its own consequences that will manifest in several different ways in your life. There will be some that are obvious, while others could be a little harder to identify. The important thing to know is that the acts can be stopped.

**Emotional Intelligence Mastery**

# Chapter 5:
# EQ Trick #1: Reading Body Language

Whether you are out with friends at the office, the body language of those around you will speak volumes. It has been suggested that body language makes up around 60% of what we communicate, so knowing how to read these non-verbal cues people send out is a very important skill. From the behavior of the eye to the direction in which a person aims their feet, body language can show you what a person actually thinks. What we are going to look at in this first EQ improving trick is finding out the ways on comprehending the body language in order to clearly perceive those around you or the ones you associate with on a daily basis. We will go over the with most common body language cues.

There are two sides to understanding a person's body language:

- Decoding is the ability you have to read other people's cues. It is the way that you interpret hidden emotions, personality, and information for a person's non-verbal cues.

- Encoding is the ability you have to send cues out to another person. This is the way in which you control your personal branding, what your first impression is that you send out, and how you make others feel when you are around them.

## Watch the Eyes

The behavior of the eyes can tell you a lot. When you are talking with somebody, pay close attention to whether or not they make direct eye contact. The inability to make direct eye contact could mean they are bored, disinterested, or are lying. The latter is true if they look away and to the side. If they look down, it often indicates they are submissive or nervous.

Also, have a look at their pupils to see if they are dilated. This will let you know if somebody is responding favorably. Pupils will dilate when their cognitive effort increases, so if they are focused on something they like, their pupils will dilate. Pupil dilation will often be difficult to detect, but with the right conditions, you should be able to notice it.

The rate at which a person blinks can tell you a lot about a person's state internally. The number of blinking a person does increase while they are busy analyzing something or someone in their thoughts and this includes them being stressed. Sometimes, increased blinking can indicate lying, especially if they start touching their face, mainly their eyes and mouth. Glancing at something can suggest that they want what they are looking at. For instance, supposing that their eyes always stray towards the direction of the door, they probably want to leave. Glancing at another person could mean they want to talk to them.

It is also suggested that when a person looks up and to the right while talking, they are telling a lie, and when they look up and to the left, this indicates that whatever they are telling you, it is devoid of falsehood. The rationale on this action is that we tend to position our heads looking upright and in the direction of the right whenever we have to use our image-making power of the mind in creating a narrative or fabricate something whereas looking onto the direction of the left signifies that one is trying to recall a real memory.

### Watch Their Face

While most people will control their facial expression, there is still a chance to pick up on important non-verbal cues if you really pay attention. Make sure you pay close attention to their mouth when you are trying to decipher their non-verbal behavior.

A simple is an action that carries a potent influence on others. Smiling is a weighty non-verbal action wherein you have to be on the lookout for. There are lots of smiles, which include fake and genuine smiles. A genuine smile will engage the entire face. A fake smile will typically only use the mouth. A genuine smile suggests that they are happy and like the company of those around them. A fake smile is meant to show approval or pleasure but also suggests that the smiler is hiding something.

A "half-smile" is another common smile that will use one side of the mouth and normally indicates uncertainty or sarcasm. You could also notice a grimace that lasts for a short second before a person smile. This normally means that they are hiding their dissatisfaction behind a fake smile.

Pursed and tight lips also show that they are displeased, while a relaxed mouth normally means they have a relaxed attitude and are in a positive mood. If a person touches their lips or mouth with their fingers or hands while they are talking could mean that they are lying.

**Pay Attention to Proximity**
Proximity refers to the distance between you and the person you are talking to. Look to see how close somebody sits or stands next to you to figure out if they favor you. Sitting or standing in close proximity is one of the best indicators of rapport. If somebody moves away or backs

up when you get closer, this could mean that you don't have a mutual connection. One can gather a lot of information about the relationship of someone to another through looking at how close they are on each other or their proximity. Remember that there are some cultures that prefer more or less distance during the interaction, so proximity isn't a foolproof indicator of an affinity to somebody.

### See If They Mirror You

Mirroring means that the person you are talking with mimics your body language. When you are interacting with somebody, check to see if they mirror your behavior. For example, if you are both sitting at a table and you place your elbow on the table, wait ten seconds to see if the other person follows suit. Another common mirroring movement involves you and them sipping drinks simultaneously. Mimicking body language signifies the desire to establish rapport. Try switching up your body posture to see if they will change theirs as well.

### Watch Their Head Movement

The speed at which somebody nods their head when you are talking will indicate how much patience they have. Slow nodding will show that they interested at what was being said verbally which therefore makes one want you to carry on whatever you're doing. Nods performed with great speed indicate that the audience wants you to stop talking because they have had enough of whatever you're spouting about.

When they tilt their head sideways while talking, it could mean they are interested in what you have to say. A backward tilt of the head can single uncertainty or suspicion. People will often use their face or head as some sort of pointers to the people that has a relationship with them or the ones, they are interested in. You should be able to notice the people who have power and the number of times other people take a glance in their direction. Conversely, the ones who aren't significant aren't looked at as often.

### Take A Look at Their Feet

One area of the body that people will "leak" non-verbal cues to are their feet. The main reason people unintentionally communicate through their feet is that they are working a lot to control their facial expressions and the position of their upper body, so important clues are revealed through the feet. Whether standing or sitting, a person will typically have their feet pointed in the direction they want to travel. If you happen to notice that a person's feet are pointed at you, this could mean they have a good opinion of you. This can apply to one-on-one interaction as well as a group interaction.

In fact, you can get a lot from a group dynamic by looking at their body language, especially the direction that their feet are pointed. In addition, if a person appears to be engaged in a conversation with you, but their feet are aimed at a different person, it's likely they would prefer to talk to that particular person, regardless of what their upper body clues could be saying.

## Watch Their Hands

Just like the feet, the hands will leak important cues when it comes to body language. This is very important when you read body language, so make sure you pay close attention to this part of the body. Be on the lookout for hand signals, like placing their hands in their pockets or placing their hand on their head. This could indicate anything from outright deception to nervousness.

Unconsciously pointing through hand gestures could speak volumes. When making gestures with their hands, a person will often point in the direction of the one they share something with. This is especially important to keep an eye out for during meetings and in group settings. Supporting their head with their hand by placing their elbow on a table could show that the person is listening and is holding their head so that they can remain focused. If they are using both elbows on the table while supporting their head, could indicate they are bored.

When a person is holding an object between them and the person they are talking with, this creates a barrier that is supposed to block out the other person. If there are two people talking and one person has a pad of paper in front of them, this is viewed as a blocking action.

## Look at Their Arm Position

View a person's arms as the doorway to their self and body. If a person has their arms crossed while talking with you, it typically is viewed as a defensive blocking gesture. Crossed arms may also show a closed mind, anxiety, or vulnerability. A crossed arm, sincere smile, and the loose way a person holds and positions their body indicate a confident attitude. Usually, a hand that is positioned in the hips signifies the desire to show that they are dominant. Men tend to do such actions as compared to women.

These clues are a great way of finding the actual hidden motivations a person has, however, these aren't infallible. In analyzing a person's body language, you have to remember that these techniques won't apply to everybody 100% of the time. There are certain factors, like culture and their general body language habits, which have to be taken into consideration to decode these non-verbal cues accurately.

Now, I'm going to throw you a curve ball. Men and women use body language slightly differently. Let's take a quick look at some the common differences so that you can use the eight points above more effectively. Women and men lie differently. They also have different motivations for deception.

Men will lie to appear more successful, interesting, and powerful. They will lie about themselves eight times more often than they lie about a different person.

Women will lie less about themselves and more to make sure that they can protect the feelings of others or to make another person feel better about themselves.

Men like to see availability over everything else. Men find availability body language more attractive. Studies have found the men are drawn towards women engaged in coquetry as this signifies her being a readily obtainable woman instead of going after the best-looking women in the room. Flirtation behavior includes:

- Leaning towards the other person.

- Intimate eye gazing.

- Keeping their hands out of their pockets.

- Minimal arm crossing.

- Having an expressive face.

- Smiling.

Men will most often point their toes towards the person that they are the most interested in. If they don't find interest in anybody, they will most likely point their toes towards the door. Female body language also comes with some difference to that of the male body language. The biggest difference between men and women is their courtship behavior. The following are a few behaviors that women will do, whether consciously or subconsciously when they are trying to attract a man:

A lot like Marilyn Monroe, women who want to attract the attention of a man will often raise the eyebrows and lower their eyelids because it looks a lot like the face women make when they experience pleasure.

Glancing up and to the side at a man they like is a common "come hither" look a woman will give.

A sideways glance over their raised shoulder will show off the curves and roundness of their face. This exposes the vulnerability of their neck, releases pheromones, and signifies estrogen. Women will often instinctively do this when they are trying to flirt with a man.

- Women will often try to divert your focus onto their lips through the use of bright and glossy lipstick.

- Women often expose their armpits through the constant touching of the neck and hair-tossing actions. As odd as this may seem, it releases sex hormones, shows the curve of the neck, and highlights their healthy hair.

- Women often struggle with standing their ground while not intimidating the other person. With body language, this can happen in several different ways. Women will often use submissiveness cues to show vulnerability, but they will also use certain assertiveness moves to show that they aren't pushovers.

- Women will pluck their eyebrows higher on their forehead because it makes them look helpless.

Limp or exposed wrists also show a sign of submission. Some people will do this subconsciously if they are in a room with a person they want to attract. This is the reason why women who smoke will hold their cigarette with their wrist turned out and exposed.

When a woman is interested in being assertive, they will stand with their feet spread apart.

## Chapter 6:
## EQ Trick #2: Releasing Destructive Emotions

Destructive emotions are emotions that cause you to do something that will harm you or somebody else. The funny thing is, nearly every emotion can be destructive, even happiness. Manic excitement can cause a person to do destructive things, but for the most part in this chapter, we are looking at depressions, paralyzing fear, and anger. Anger is the biggie that people face, which has a chapter all on its own later in the book.

Being happy with your life is controlled by your own mind and nothing else. The mind is the main obstacle to happiness, or, really, anything. The biggest obstacles we face when it comes to happiness and living a peaceful and fulfilling life are our own tendencies to be afflicted by emotions such as jealousy, envy, hatred, and anger, which are the real enemies of well-being.

Daniel Goleman, if you remember him from earlier in the book, went so far as to talk to the Dalai Lama about these destructive emotions. The takeaway from this chapter and their meeting was that understanding our destructive emotions and understanding that we can free ourselves from them, is going to help us to handle these types of emotions with confidence. There are some people out there that could argue that we are hardwired and directed by biology and that these types of emotions are just a part of our nature. They probably feel as if we can't do anything about them. So, do we have to remain a slave to our biological instincts?

Let's take anger, for example. From an evolutionary standpoint, it serves a purpose. It helped out ancestors to survive. Anger is an appropriate response to injustice or a wrong that should be righted. If you want to respond effectively in response to what causes you to feel angry, you have to keep the energy and focus of anger but get rid of the anger itself so that you can act skillfully.

Every religion has long viewed human beings as possessing the capacity to change from within. The Indic spiritual traditions are full of these types of success stories. The Valmiki changed from hunters to Sanskrit scholars. The Angelical went from cruel dacoit to followers of Buddha. Tulsidas changed from a lustful layman to a great Sanskrit poet.

## Stephen Patterson

Recent findings looking into brain plasticity has found that nothing is created in stone. Changes can happen. Brain patterns can and will change with time in response to our experiences and thoughts. In order to stay emotionally fine with others and ourselves, we have to understand and work with the negative emotions we experience in a conscious manner and train ourselves to reach a positive transformation.

Biologically, our basic emotions had an evolutionary purpose. The attachment will bring us together and form bonds, which gives us a society and family. Anger pushes back harmful forces that are detrimental to survival. Fear will help alert us to threats. Envy will prompt us to compete with others so that we can do better, which will bring about progress. From a scientific viewpoint, these emotions do have a bit of a positive aspect and biological purpose as long as we don't allow them to spiral out of control.

Emotions have dual aspects. Every emotion can be non-destructive and destructive. Going back to the anger example, anger can be channeled to help you get things done and reach what you rightly seek. If you allow it to go beyond this practical function, it will become destructive then it becomes violence. Gandhi understood this practical function of anger and used it in a positive way to reach political and freedom reform. Similarly, doubt will allow us to seek out answers and to improve our understanding, but if we allow it to become pathological, it will paralyze us and prevent us from taking any form of decisive action. Competition, as long as it isn't ego driven, can be constructive and will lead to progress.

After we are able to recognize the destructive sides of all emotions, we will be more cautious. This will then allow us to become more emotionally aware. We must be attentive in our behavior at the level of speech, body, and most definitely, mind. Our first effort should be to make sure that our destructive emotions aren't displayed through our body language. This will keep any chance of an angry explosion to be stopped. Then, you will be able to reach the source of the arising emotion. Now, you could possibly reinterpret the thought that triggered your emotion in a positive way. Having this awareness will guard you against instinctive interpretations that are clouded by projection and exaggeration, thus you will be able to respond calmly.

## Meditation

The first practice you can use to help control your destructive emotions is meditation. The effects of meditation can easily be seen in Buddhist monks. They have their entire day to meditate if they want, so people may think that it's not possible to reap the benefits of meditation because they don't have the time to meditate. That's not true.

Research has started to look at the effects of mediation on beginners. They can see the beginnings of similar shifts in people who have only been meditating for two months. Another study took highly stressed workers at a tech firm and taught them to meditate. The researchers discovered that they changed the set point of the brain from the "distressed zone" to the "good zone." That was only after two months of meditating for an hour each day.

The key is, though, daily meditation. Most people probably don't have time for an hour-long daily meditation session, and that's okay. Five minutes is enough to help control your mind so that you aren't overtaken by destructive emotions. Meditation is important because we are normally afraid of looking at our reality. We are all afraid that if we allow our self to come face to face with who we are, all of our illusions about who we are will fall away. Through meditation, you will be able to turn the energy in you into an inner force. Emotions are simply inner electricity.

**Acceptance and Awareness**

There are two steps in this process: acceptance and awareness. Yep, it's that easy. First off, you need to really accept that emotion is there. That at that moment you feel anger or sadness, and then you can use that energy. This is where relaxation happens. You will stop fighting your emotions. In this relaxation, awareness of the mechanism of your unconscious can be used. This awareness will automatically transform because you knowingly can't be angry, knowingly you aren't able to be greedy. For violence, greed, or anger, unawareness is required. Just like you can't knowingly drink poison. Just like you can't knowingly place your hand in a flame. You aren't able to be knowingly angry. Once you are aware of that anger, it's lost its power.

The most important key to acceptance is that you don't have any condemnation or rejection of the emotion that is there. You shouldn't have an interpretation of whether it's bad or good, you just acknowledge and accept whatever you have there in that particular moment. While this may sound easy, it won't be all that easy in practice. It's hard to acknowledge and see what it is without commenting or judging it. This is where meditation can help. Your brain will learn how to do this through mindfulness meditation.

It's important to note, though, that acceptance doesn't mean resignation. Acceptance simply meant that you accept the fact that the emotion is there. Notice that envy is present and acknowledge it. Be aware of what is happening and watch it. It's an amazing phenomenon to witness energy moving through you. It's a lot like electricity in the clouds. Primitive people used to fear lightning. Then science discovered how to change that electricity into energy that could run an air conditioner, a fridge, whatever you need it to. The electricity from lightning has now become a domestic force, and it is no longer seen as anger or viewed as a threat.

The moment you can channel your emotions, be it anger, envy, what have you, it will become your servant. Anger is only energy, and if you can't understand that, you will end up becoming mad. If you understand that, you will be able to transform the energy and use it in a creative way. The emotions energy will always be there. It's whether you use them, or you allow them to use you.

Remember, the only way you be aware of the emotion is to fully accept it first. If you don't allow yourself to accept the emotion completely, you will try to avoid it in little ways. You will start to think of something else to do, or you try to pretend that it's not there. You will end up building a façade, or you will try to justify it in some way. This will lead you to a dead end.

Your goal isn't to repress. This isn't the goal of meditation or accept and acknowledge. You want to watch your destructive emotions in both situations. There is a huge difference. Neither of these practices should have you sitting on top of your destructive emotions, ignore it, nor do something against it. It's not that when you are upset you should smile. That would be a false smile. Instead, shut the door and sit with that destructive emotion. You don't even have to show it to anybody. It is only your business and your energy. Keep watching it. You will quickly realize that the destructive emotion is not able to be there forever. If you don't do anything to control it, what is going to happen? Is that emotion able to hang forever and ever? Nothing is able to hang around forever. Happiness even comes and goes. All things change, and nothing stays permanent. Let that negative emotion be, watch it, and it will leave. This is the goal of both practices.

If you make sure that you don't act on or repress the destructive emotion, you will quickly notice that you will become calmer and your energy will change. Don't try to force this change. It will come when it is meant to. This is the secret to transforming your hot electricity into air conditioning.

## Chapter 7:
## EQ Trick #3: Develop Social-Awareness

Social awareness is what gives you the ability to respond and understand the needs of those around you. When you improve your social skill, you will gain the respect of others. Being able to understand other people's feelings is imperative to emotional intelligence. If you get another person's emotions wrong and you will be viewed as insensitive and uncaring. You know the basic capabilities of emotional intelligence, and guess what; social awareness is one of them. Social awareness includes:

- The waiter who suggests something different on the menu to you.

- The salesperson that goes a step further.

- A supportive team leader.

- The executive who always remembers your name.

- All of these people have great social awareness skills. The competencies that come along with good social awareness are:

- Empathy: This means that you are able to understand another person's concerns, emotions, and needs.

- Organizational Awareness: This is the ability to understand the politics of an organization and how it affects the people that work in the organization.

- Service: This is the ability to meet and understand the needs of customers and clients.

Having awareness in social situations means that you are careful to consider what the other person wants, and you plan on communicating with them in such a way that will help to meet that need. Whether this is the same as manipulation is unseen. Public speakers and great leaders have amazing skills in social awareness. It will help them to build up support. Social awareness isn't calculated like manipulation is. At best, social awareness is a natural response to those around you where you take their needs and situation into account as much as you can.

Reports from *Scientific American* suggests that our empathy levels have lowered over the past 30 years. Having an increase in social isolation may be a theory as to why empathy has reduced. Video conferencing, social networking, digital communication, and other forms of media contributes to the problem of social isolation and tend to be the blame of lower empathy.

After all, it is a lot easier to say mean things about another person if you don't have to see them. To avoid becoming tangled with somebody else's problems, you can simply log off or unfriend them. It's a really easy option. The problem when empathy is lost, when we can't work to understand another person's needs, the trust will be lost.

If I can't figure out what you are feeling and thinking, I am going to trust you less and isolate myself. This can end up having a lot of implications for businesses where trust is the key to successful partnerships and leadership.

More importantly, when you are able to respond to the feelings and needs of others, you will gain their trust. Other people are going to be seen as insensitive and uncaring, but you will be trusted when you can respond and understand their values and needs. This is true whether you are a salesperson who has to deal with the public or an organization leader.

Empathy is a big part of social awareness, but in the next chapter we will deal with empathy specifically, so I won't go into great detail about it here. One thing I will touch on, in reference to empathy, is can you be too empathic?

Your ability to be able to understand and connect with others is very important, but it is also important to be able to control this so that it doesn't end up becoming a burden. There are some people who find it super easy to empathize with others, and this is always appreciated. The problem is that you can get over-involved in the problems of others and it can end up leading to emotional exhaustion. While you are looking out for the emotions of others, you will forget to look after your emotions.

This isn't being emotionally intelligent. If you find that this happens to you, a lot, then it's probably a good idea to transform your empathy into something that you can control.

Alright, let's look at a few ways to build social awareness:

- Improve how well you listen. Look into what effective communication means.

- Make sure that you pay close attention to how you interact with people. Be aware of the things that the other person says, how they say it, and how they act.

- Self-hypnosis videos can help a person to understand other people better.

- Try to identify the emotional states of other people. Listen very closely to what they say and take notice of the way they respond to external things, like somebody saying hello or asking them to do something for them.

- Take notice of your feelings. How are the other person's emotions making you feel?

- Think completely before you provide an answer and make sure that your answers are clear.

- Here is an exercise you can try the next time you are in a social situation. Pay close attention to how you interact with the other person. Ask these questions.

- Was I actively listening to the person who came up to me? Was I too busy to let them talk to me?

- Did I ask them questions about what they were talking about as well as questions about their emotions and feelings about what they were talking about?

- Did I allow my body language, the tone of voice, facial expressions, and other non-verbal communication elements change in order to meet that person's need?

Being socially aware is what will affect your response to situations and people. The starting place to become socially aware is to make sure you are self-aware. Self-awareness is important so that you can understand the emotions and feelings of others while self-management is needed to make sure that you respond appropriately in a given situation.

To give an empathic response will require that you are aware of the diversity and the sensitivity to the emotions and needs of others. Diversity includes response and acceptance while also noticing your own uniqueness and differences. Open communication plays a big role in managing diversity and creating awareness when you are in a social situation.

"Everything starts with an 'E'." Everything may start with the letter 'E', but the word empathy, I've found, starts with 'U'. Mother Teresa even explained that empathy begins with us. She said, "Do not wait for leaders; do it alone, person to person." Remember this advice because it comes from one of the top voices of social awareness.

Social awareness is important to your emotional intelligence. You shouldn't complain about a person not understanding your needs. Focus instead on expanding your emotional intelligence and make sure that you practice empathy, organization awareness, and be on service to others. According to Stephen Covey, "Seek first to understand, then to be understood."

The more you practice this, the more likely this will become a habit. As you work to improve social awareness, you will improve your experience life make better opportunities in your work-life balance, develop your personal radar when it comes to perceiving what other people are feeling, and promote the growth of your skills in answer to random and sudden events.

**Emotional Intelligence Mastery**

# Chapter 8:
# EQ Trick #4: Building Empathy

A simple definition of empathy is being able to understand and share other people's emotions and feelings. You need empathy to be able to have good relationships in your personal life and at work. People who don't show empathy are thought of as self-absorbed and cold. They usually lead isolated lives. Empathy is the main component in emotional intelligence and helps people succeed within their profession. Empathy can help develop many levels of trust and rapport. Sociopaths usually don't have any empathy. A person who has empathy is thought to be caring and warm.

If you have poor empathy skills it could lead to some bad consequences. It could cause conflict from not being able to understand. Without empathy, we might feel lonely even if we have a relationship. Having a lack of empathy could cause businesses to make mistakes that might alienate employees and customers. It might even cause violence.

**Importance of Empathy**

Studies that have been done at hospitals in Massachusetts showed physicians who were empathic forged stronger relationships with their patients. Their patients were more satisfied. Their patients responded to treatments better. They also had fewer medical errors. Empathy is important in the workplace, too. Empathy is related to better job performance. Empathic managers were looked at as better workers by their bosses.

## Brains and Empathy

Neuroscientists have discovered that humans experience empathy through systems of mirror neurons that are located in our brains. When we see other people's actions, these mirror neurons reflect these actions and we will mimic their actions. If we see someone in pain or if we are with people who are happy, we will experience those feelings, as well. The mirror neurons are the basis for empathy. They make a Wi-Fi connection from us to the feelings of others around us. Some people are just naturally empathic. Some aren't. Good news is empathy can be learned. The bad news is there are some roadblocks to learning empathy that some might have to overcome.

## Overcoming Roadblocks

Our mirror neurons get stronger when we see other people's emotions. We can see their gestures, body position, eye expressions, and facial expressions. We might not have the motivation to pay attention to others or we might be distracted by other things or our own thoughts while we try to multitask.

Solution: You have to motivate yourself to be empathic by knowing empathy is important to success at work and home. Put away your computer and cell phones to minimize distractions. Research active listening and learn to practice it. Improve your observation skills. Learn how to read eyes and facial expressions. If we can learn to be more attentive, we will be able to sense others inner states.

Turn on the television but mute the volume. Now practice nonverbal interpretation by trying to read what the characters are talking about and feeling. This will be best done by watching subtle dramas and not action movies.

## Feeling Emotions but Not Knowing When to Communicate Empathy

Solution: You have to increase your awareness of nonverbal expressions. Figure out what you do nonverbally with you interact with others. Find people you trust and ask them to give you honest feedback about the way you communicate nonverbally in different situations. Focus on ones that are emotional.

Figure out who you have problems being empathic with. Try to figure out why. Learn about voice tone. Listen to people who are empathic friends, teachers, leaders, or possibly interviewers. See how they use their voice to show empathy. Repeat this sentence: "I'm sorry this happened to you," different ways with different voice tones. Figure out if you can tell which way sounds empathic or ask others to help you out.

Realize that there are many situations where it might not be good to respond with empathy, like when someone is sending signals that they aren't wanting to interact with you or they aren't wanting to share their feelings with you.

**Cognitive Empathy.**
You aren't feeling the same emotions as others around you. But you know that you should communicate with them empathically.

Solution: It is okay to disagree with people but still understand what they are feeling and why they are having these feelings. This is very important when somebody has strong emotions and asks you to do things you don't want to do. Sometimes if you can listen without judging it is enough to show empathy. Communicate to them in a true way that you know what they are going through.

## Faking Empathy

It might be necessary at times to act empathically in order to achieve a certain outcome even if you feel bitter towards the person. Take for example hostage negotiators. These people are trained to act with empathy toward the kidnapper, so you can establish a rapport with them. You have to talk them into giving themselves up without hurting anyone. The negotiator deep down probably feels hate or disgust toward the kidnapper because they are hiding behind a woman with a baby. It is interesting to watch that in a couple of hours some negotiators will begin to feel empathy toward the kidnapper because they have been "acting" empathic. Many people aren't ever going to be in that position, but you might have to fake empathy to influence others. You might not experience that often since there is a price you have to pay for being fake all the time.

Empathy is a building block to social intelligence. Lack of time, self-absorption, and stress can build up and kill empathy. You need to know what your roadblocks are and explore different ways to overcome them could help you create tools that will help you succeed at work and home.

Since research has shown that empathy is partly learned and partly natural. Anyone can improve. Here are some ways you can strengthen your empathy:

- Challenge yourself: Do challenges experiences that push you outside your zone of comfort. Learn new skills like a foreign language, new hobby, or musical instrument. Learn a new skill within your profession. Do things that will make you humble as humility is the key to empathy.

- Change your environment: If at all possible, travel to new cultures and places. It will help you appreciate others better.

- Ask for feedback: Ask colleagues, friends, and family for feedback about your relationship skills. Check in with them from time to time to see if you are improving.

- Explore your heart not your head: Read books, magazines, and articles about emotions and relationships. This can help to improve empathy in residences.

- Walk in other people's shoes: Talk to people about what they are having problems with. Ask them about their concerns and issues and what they thought about your experiences.

- Look at your biases: Everyone has hidden biases. Sometimes these biases aren't as hidden as they think they are. These biases can interfere with our ability to empathize and listen. These are usually centered around factors like gender, race, and age. If you don't think you have biases, check yourself, most people do.

- Work on your curiosity: Can you learn anything from an inexperienced colleague? Can you learn anything from a client who has a narrow view? People who are curious will ask a lot of questions that will lead them to create a better understanding of people who around them.

- Ask more questions: When you have meetings with colleagues or clients, bring three or four provocative questions with you.

Emotional Intelligence Mastery

## Chapter 9:
## EQ Trick #5: Handing Conflicts the Right Way

Is there a right way to handle conflicts? What happens if you handle it poorly? There will always be conflict in the workplace because employees will have different opinions, goals, and personalities. Learning how to effectively handle conflicts is necessary for anybody in management. It is the key to preventing it from hurting employee's growth.

In order to manage conflict, you have to be a skilled communicator. This means you need to create an open environment by encouraging your employees to talk to you about problems. When you listen to your employee's concerns, it will create a welcoming environment. Make certain that the employees are understood whatever their concerns are through enquiring them and zero in your attention to the way they perceive the problem. It doesn't matter if you have two or two hundred employees if they are having problems you need to know how to handle it. You might have two employees who are fighting for the desk that is next to a window or an employee who wants the heat turned up and another one who doesn't. Your response to these situations is critical.

Here are some tips to use when facing employees who can't resolve their own problems:

### Realize A Problem Exists.
Each party needs to be honest. There also needs to be clear lines of communication to be able to resolve the problem. Familiarize yourself with what is happening and be open.

### Find the Cause of The Conflict.
What problem was reported? What negative impact did it cause on the relationship or workplace? Do the involved parties have differing personalities? Meet with each party separately and then together.

You need to have all the information about the conflict, so you can resolve it quickly. To find the information you need, you need to ask questions such as, "How did this start?" "Can you see a relationship between specific problems?" "When did you get upset?" Being a supervisor or manager, you have to get both sides to the story. It will help you understand the situation better and show that you are impartial. As you listen to each employee, say, "I see" or "I understand" to show you understand and encourage them to continue talking.

**Look Beyond A Specific Incident.**
Most of the time it isn't a situation but the way the situation was perceived that causes the anger and leads to shouting or other problems that show a conflict.

The source might be a small problem that happened months before. The stress grew to a point where employees started attacking one another instead of addressing the main problem. Inside your calm office, you can get them to look farther than the incident to the true cause. Again, use questions such as: "When do you think this problem between the two of you began?" "What do you think happened here?" Feelings of hurt or anger go along with conflicts. Before you can begin any problem solving, you have to let them acknowledge and express these emotions.

**Ask for Solutions.**
After you have gotten everyone's viewpoint about the conflict, now you have to ask each party how they situation might be changed. You have to ask them again to give you some ideas: "How can I help you make things better?"

You aren't deciding who is right or wrong. You are trying to reach a solution that each party can live with. Look for needs instead of solutions. This will generate winning options. To find needs, you have to figure out why people want the solutions they proposed. When you understand the advantages, these solutions will give them, you know their needs.

As a mediator, you have to know how to listen, be aware of each nuance, and be able to read body language. All you have to do is listen. You need to get the disputants to quit fighting and begin cooperating. This means you have to steer the discussion away from pointing fingers and to a way to resolve the conflict.

### Find Solutions Both Parties Agree On.

You have been listening to an acceptable course of action. Give merit to different ideas from everyone's perspective, but also that will benefit the organization. Finding solutions that will satisfy everyone's needs:

- Solve the problem by finding multiple alternatives.
- Decide what actions will be taken.
- Be sure all parties agree on the actions.
- Make sure you get agreement from everybody.

### Agreement

Once everyone has agreed on everything, get the parties to shake hands and agree on alternatives that were found in the above step. Some mediators will write up a contract where actions and time frames are finalized. It might be enough to have the parties involved answer these questions: "What action plans will you both put in place to keep conflicts from happening in the future?" and "What will you do if problems arise in the future?"

Find common areas to agree on and it doesn't matter how small they may be:

- Agree on a small change for success.
- Agree on fears.
- Agree on following the procedure.
- Agree of the problem.

### Follow Up to Monitor Actions.

You should schedule a meeting about two weeks after the incident to see how the parties are doing. If the conflict doesn't get resolved, you might have to explore other options. Bringing in an outside mediator might bring some insights into solving the problem. In many cases, the conflict will become a performance issue and might be a topic for coaching sessions, disciplinary action, or performance appraisals. This process will work with groups as well.

# Chapter 10:
# EQ Trick #6: Asking Critical Questions

The way to think better is to question more. If you learn to ask the correct questions, you will be a better thinker. Questions are the force behind our thinking. Thinking can cause your mind to veer in many different directions and some of them will be dead ends. Questions hold the agenda to what we think about. They are essentially the information we are looking for. They will take us in a specific direction instead of everywhere. They are an absolutely essential part of thinking.

### A Key to Critical Questioning
One essential thing that is basic to critical thinking is based on the basic structures of thinking. Another one is based on the fundamental standards of thinking. From these foundations, we should be able to come up with powerful questions for us to ask. Questions need to help us get to the foundation of thinking and to begin to figure out our weaknesses and strengths. Let's talk about the elements of thought. These are the structures of a person's thinking as they go along life's path. If you are

thinking about anything, you are using these structures. They are created by each act of thinking.

## Elements of Thought

These elements are as important to thinking as the elements that make up every substance. If we don't know the basics of chemistry, we can't check, examine, and identify building blocks and therefore can't do chemistry. If we don't know the basics of thinking, we can't check, examine, and identify the building blocks and therefore can't critically think.

## Breaking Down Thinking

To develop critical thinking, you have to take your thinking apart and understand its elements. Understanding these elements isn't just memorizing definitions. Instead, it is understanding all the functions that thinking includes. Just like the human body is made up of the respiratory, cardiovascular, nervous systems, etc. a thinker is made up of interrelated elements as well.

## The Elements Numbered

Let's think about these elements. Humans think for a purpose. We usually have some sort of goal, motivation, or an end we are looking for.

When we pursue a purpose, we generate questions. In order to answer these questions, you need some information. In order to use this information, you have to be able to make sense of it. In order to make sense of this information, you have to make some conclusions and inferences. In order to make inferences, you have to use concepts. In order to use concepts, you have to make assumptions. In order to make assumptions that will lead to inferences that lead to consequences and implications. And last but not least, we need to think with purpose, using the information that we have found, to make conclusions within a certain viewpoint. Here are some examples:

Let's say you want to get a better job. You have questions that are important to this purpose. Are there any jobs out there that I am qualified to do and would like to do? What disadvantages and advantages do these jobs offer? How is the best way to apply for these jobs that interest me?

After these questions are clear to you, it is easy to realize that you need to gather some information about these jobs.

After you have gathered the information, you will need to come to certain conclusions about these potential jobs such as: which are the best options and how can I go about getting these options.

In trying to figure out these options you will have to make certain assumptions about what you are qualified to do, the job's nature, and will you be satisfied with this job.

Your thinking will generate certain implications that you should think about: the implications of being out of work for some time, the implications of losing seniority, having a longer commute to and from work, will it impact your family.

While thinking you need to look at the idea of improving your quality of life by improving your job. You need to be sure you aren't assuming a job change is going to make your life better or what problems you are having will be helped by taking another job.

You need to think about your point of view when thinking about changing jobs. How are you looking at your circumstances? How are you envisioning this change? Is your viewpoint realistic? Is this relative to your objective? Are there other points you need to think about? What if the new job is in a different city, will my wife want to move?

This is just an example. If you were really thinking about a job change, there need to be a lot of specifics and details incorporated into your thinking. It really doesn't matter, once you are comfortable with and have practices evaluating and analyzing the structures of thought, they can become a powerful guide for generating useful questions. You might find that you are frequently questioning things in these categories:

- What are your agenda, goal, or purpose?

- What is the main question you need to answer?

- What problem do I need to solve?

- Is there a critical issue you have to resolve?

- What information do you need to answer these questions?

- What information do I need to solve the problem?

- What information do I need to resolve the critical issue?

- With the information you have available to you, what conclusions can you make?

- How should I interpret the information that I have found?

- What is the main idea or concept that you need to know to understand the data and be able to resolve the issue, solve the problem, or answer the question?

- As you are thinking about the issue, problem or question, what are you assuming or taking for granted?

- Are you justified?

- Thinking about what you have reasoned through so far, what does your reasoning say to you?

- If you act on your conclusions, what would the consequences be?

- Are you approaching the issue, problem or question from the right point of view?

- Do you need to think about a different point of view?

As you use these strategies in all the aspects of your life, you might find features in your thinking that should be changed, reconstructed, and rethought. You might realize that the goals and purposes that have been buried in your behavior should be questioned. You might find that you are unclear about the problems and questions that you want to be clearer about. You will see that when you put the problems and questions in a precise and clear form, you will be able to answer and solve them. Once the main question is clearly in your mind, the information that is relevant to your questions will be clear.

You will explicitly seek out what information you need. As you look for the information, you will see that you are looking at the information closer and judging it more. Once you are clear about the information, you will be clearer about the conclusions you come to as based on the information. When these relationships are clear, other relationships will get clearer, too. Once you realize that you are coming to a certain conclusion, you will also see that you are making an assumption using one or more ideas. Knowing that you are engaged with the total you will see that you are thinking in a viewpoint. Basically, the process of just questioning the basics of your thinking will improve your thinking. The more you practice, the better you get.

When you question the information, you are using to come to conclusions about events and people in your life, you might discover that you don't have enough information to make good conclusions. You might come to conclusions anyway. Then you might realize you made a mistake and then have to question the conclusions. You have to take them out of the "fact" column and put them into the guess category.

Realizing that you don't have enough information to use, you need to question your motives. You need to ask if you have a self-centered motive for the conclusion. Let's say somebody made you angry. You might find yourself making negative conclusions about that person at another time without having good reasons. You will then realize that you are letting your self-centered tendencies take control. You can then change.

## Using Explicit Standards to Judge Thinking

While you are developing your critical thinking, you have to take your thinking apart and understand its elements. You have to questions these elements using explicit standards. Understanding the standards for thought doesn't mean you have to memorize a bunch of definitions. Instead, it is just understanding another set of standards that turns thinking into sound thinking.

Humans have been judging thinking for over a thousand years but haven't spent time learning the criteria to use in figuring out what to reject or accept which ones to criticize and which ones to praise. When we see that the human mind is prone to self-deception and using that thinking in a self-serving way. It shouldn't surprise us that the standards that we use to think aren't just flawed intellectually but actually absurd. We have the following criteria in mind:

- "It is true because you believe it." This is natural egocentrism. You might find that you constantly assume that what you think is true even though you haven't questioned the basis of your beliefs.

- "It is true because we believe it." This is natural sociocentrism. You might find yourself constantly assuming that the group's beliefs are true even though you've never questioned any of these beliefs.

- "It is true because you want to believe it." This is a natural wish fulfillment. You might find yourself believing in a positive instead of a negative even though you haven't looked for any evidence for the negative account. You believe in what "feels good," what supports your beliefs, what doesn't need you to change your thinking drastically, what doesn't make you admit you were wrong.

- It is true because you have always believed it." This is natural self-validation. You feel a strong attraction to beliefs that you have held but haven't considered the evidence to critique these beliefs.

- "It is true because it is in my absolute interest to believe it." This is natural selfishness. You find yourself drawn to beliefs that if they are true would help you get more power, personal advantage, and money. You won't notice the reasoning against these beliefs.

If we agree that humans naturally assess thinking by the above criteria, this it shouldn't surprise us that we haven't developed an interest in teaching intellectual standards. There are many aspects of our thinking that we don't want to be questioned. We hold onto too many prejudices that we don't want to be challenged. We want to have our absolute interests served. We aren't concerned about protecting the rights of others. We won't sacrifice out desires to help someone else's needs. We don't want to find out that our beliefs that we think is sacred or obvious may not be either. We ignore all types of principles to enable us to keep our power or to gain an advantage or more power.

## Chapter 11:
## EQ Trick #7: Forgiving Your Past

Everybody's been hurt. There isn't an adult or teen who is alive today that hasn't had some sort of emotional pain. It hurts. It's understandable. What you actually do with the hurt is more important than the actual hurt. Do you want to get back to living life? Would you rather ruminate constantly about what happened in the past and what can't be changed? Basically, we are asking how you can let go of all the hurt from the past and move on. Let's figure out how that is possible.

Most humans will begin by blaming others for the hurt. Someone did something bad or they did you wrong in a certain way. We expect an apology. They have to know what they did wrong. Blaming others for our hurt could actually backfire. When you blame others, it could leave you powerless. Let's say you confront someone, and they reply with either "So what?" or "No, I didn't", you are left with all the pent-up hurt and anger without a resolution.

Yes, your feelings are legitimate. You need to completely feel them and then move on. Feeding these grievances all the time is a horrible habit as it could potentially hurt you more than it is hurting them. When you hold onto these hurts you are just reliving the pain over and over again. You might even get stuck in this blame, hurt, or pain. The best way you can bring happiness and joy back into your life is to make room for it. If your heart is completely full of hurt and pain, it isn't going to be open for anything new. Here are some ways to help you let go of past hurts:

## Make A Decision of Letting Go

Things aren't going to go away on their own. You have to make a commitment and let them go. You might end up sabotaging all efforts to move away from this hurt if you can't make a conscious choice. Making a decision to let it go basically means that you have a "choice" to let it go. Instead of continuously reliving the past, to stop replaying the details of what happened in your head each time you see or think about this person. This will empower most people, knowing they can either hold onto the pain or live a fulfilled life without it.

## Express Your Responsibility and Pain

Express the pain you are feeling. It might be to the person who wronged you or by writing that person a letter that you won't ever send, writing it down in a journal, or venting to a close friend. Get all of it out of your system. Doing this will help you figure out what your hurt is about specifically.

Our world is not one of black of white, even though sometimes it feels that way. You might not have a whole lot of responsibility for the hurt you are feeling, but you might have a little responsibility for a small part of that hurt. Could you have done something different? Do you want to be an active participant in your life or only a victim? Is this pain going to become who you are now? Could you be more complex and deeper than that?

### Quit Blaming Others and Playing the Victim
You might think that being a victim feels pretty good. It is like being on a team of you fighting the world. Guess what? The world really doesn't care, you need to get over it. You are special. Your feelings do matter. Don't confuse the two. Don't mix up "your feelings matter" to "your feeling has to override everything else, and that is all that matters." Feelings are only one part of your life. Our lives are complex, interwoven, and messy.

Every moment of every day, you have a choice to either feel bad about other's actions or begin to feel good. You are responsible for your happiness. Stop putting all the power in other people's hands. Why let the people who have hurt you have this kind of power? There isn't any amount of analysis that has ever fixed relationship problems. It hasn't ever happened, and it never will. Why should you take part in this kind of thinking and devote all that energy into a person who you think wronged you?

## Stay Focused on The Present

You need to let it go, now. Stop reliving the past and let it go. Stop re-telling the story where you are the protagonist and the victim of this person's actions forever. The past can't be undone. You just need to make today the best day possible.

Once you can learn to focus on the here and now, you won't have time to think about the past. When your past memories do come into your mind, acknowledge them and let them go. Bring yourself back into the present gently. Some find it easy to do by using a conscious cue like saying: "I'm fine. That's the past, for now, I will focus on my happiness." If we crowd our lives and minds with hurt feelings, there won't be room for positive things. You are making a choice to feel hurt instead of bringing joy into your life.

### Stephen Patterson

## Forgive Yourself and Them

We might not have to capability to forget other's bad behavior, but everyone deserves forgiveness. We can sometimes get stuck in our stubbornness and pain, so forgiveness isn't even in our vocabulary. Forgiving someone isn't saying that you agree with what they did. Instead, you are saying that you aren't agreeing with what they did but you are going to forgive them anyway.

Forgiving others doesn't mean you are weak. It is saying that you are a good person and you are acknowledging the other person is good as well even though they hurt you. You are willing to move forward in your life and want to bring joy back into it. You can't do that until you let the hurt go.

Forgiveness means you are physically letting things go. It is showing empathy for the other person and seeing things from their viewpoint. Forgiving yourself is another part of this, too. We will sometimes blame ourselves for getting hurt. We might have a small part in the hurt but there isn't any reason for you to beat yourself up. If you can't show forgiveness to yourself, how can you live a life of happiness and peace?

## Sum It Up

Yes, this is hard to do. It is hard to let go of the pain. Most everyone alive has to struggle with this. If it is something you have held onto for a long time, it begins to feel comfortable like a friend. You just can't let it go.

No one's life needs to be defined by their pain. It isn't healthy, and it only adds to our stress. It will hurt our ability to work, study, and focus. It will impact all other relationship that we try to have. Each day that you choose to keep the pain inside is a day that everyone that you are around is living with too. You will feel its consequences. Do everyone include yourself a favor. "Let go of the pain." Try something new and bring the happiness back.

## Chapter 12:
## EQ Trick #8: Learn to Forgive

You have to forgive others to help your spiritual growth. The experience of being hurt by someone is painful but it isn't anything more than just a feeling or thought that you carry with you. If you let thoughts of hatred, anger, and resentment take up space in your head, these energies will drain your power. If you can learn to let them go, you will finally have peace. Here are 15 steps that will help you forgive somebody that has hurt you.

### Step 1: Move On
Past hurts along with your history aren't here in the physical reality any longer. Don't let them stay in your mind to mess up your present. Your life is similar to a play with many acts. Some characters that have a role only have short ones, while others will have larger ones. Some will be the good guy's others the villains. All of them are necessary or they wouldn't be in your play. Feel them, embrace them, but keep moving forward to the next act.

## Step 2: Reconnect to A Higher Power

Create an arrangement with yourself that you will always remain connected to whatever Higher Power you believe in. It might seem like the hardest thing in the world to do. If you can do this, you will bring a degree of harmony into your life. Turn your hurts over to your Higher Power and let their Spirit flow through.

This new agreement you've made with your physical self, personality, and spiritual self will start radiating a higher energy of light and love. It doesn't matter where you go, others will see your glow and any problems or disorders will not continue in your presence. You need to become "an instrument of thy peace" to quote St. Francis.

## Step 3: Never Sleep When You Are Angry

Every night, as you go to sleep, don't use this time to think about anything that you didn't want to think about when you were awake. Choose to bring forward in your mind the way you view yourself as a Divine creature being totally aligned with the Creator. Tell yourself why you are important and remember those as you drift off. Repeat to yourself these sentences: "I am love." "I am content." "I connect to those who are in the same mindset as me."

Make this a nightly ritual. Get rid of all temptations to remember any unpleasantness or fear that your ego might ask you to look at. Just remember and repeat the above "I am" statements and know that you are programming your body while you are sleeping. You will wake up the next day knowing you are free. To quote Neville Goddard: "In sleep, man impresses the subconscious mind with his conception of himself."

### Step 4: Stop Focusing Others and Understand Yourself

When you become upset over something that others did stop focusing on them and what is causing your distress. Turn your mental energy and let yourself be with what you might be feeling. Allow the experience to be as it is and don't blame other people for your feelings. Don't turn the blame on yourself either. Let the experience play out and remember that nobody can make you feel bad without your consent. You aren't giving anybody that authority.

You can experience your emotions without labeling them as "bad" or chasing them away. By doing this, you have shifted to mastering self. You have to bypass the blame and the desire to understand others. Just focus on knowing yourself. When you take responsibility for the way you respond to everybody and everything, you will align yourself with life's dance. When you change the way, you see the power other might have over you then you will see a whole new world of untapped potential for yourself. You will instantly know the way to let go and forgive anyone and anything.

## Step 5: Don't Tell People What to Do

Stay away from activities and thoughts that cause you to tell others what to do. People are very capable of making their own decisions. Remember that you are not the owner of anyone, and this means family. To quote the poet Kahlil Gibran: "Your children are not your children. They are the sons and daughters of Life's longing for itself. They come through you but not from you."

This will always hold true. Disregard any thoughts of being dominate in any relationship. Listen instead of explaining. Watch yourself when you have opinions and see where your attention takes you. If you can replace your ownership mentality with on that allows, you will see the unfolding of Tao in others and yourself. Once you have done that, you will stop being frustrated by those who don't do what you think they should.

## Step 6: Be Water

Instead of trying to dominate by forcefulness, be like water. Flow anywhere there is an opening. Let your edges soften by being tolerant of others opinions. Don't interfere and listen instead of telling and directing. If someone offers you their point of view, try to respond with "I haven't thought about that in that way, thank you. I'll think about it."

Picture yourself as being like water. Let your fluid, yielding, weak, and soft self-go into places where you would normally stay away from because you thought you were hard and unyielding. Flow freely and softly into people's lives where you once felt conflicted. Visualize yourself going into the private inner selves, possibly seeing what they are experiencing. If you can keep visualizing yourself as gentle flowing water, it won't take long before you see your relationships change.

## Step 7: Take Responsibility

Taking away blame means that you won't ever give another person the responsibility for what you might be experiencing. This means that you can say: "I might not understand why I am feeling like this, why I am sick, why I was victimized, or why I was in that accident, but I can say without guilt or resentment that it is mine. I live with, and I am responsible for it being in my life."

When you can learn to take responsibility for a specific experience, then you have a chance to take responsibility for learning from and removing it. If you are responsible for your headache or feeling depressed, then you can try to remove it or figure out what message it has for you. If you think something or someone else is responsible, then you will have to wait until they change before you can get better. This probably won't happen. You will be left with nothing and go home with nothing when you could have found peace around the corner.

### Step 8: Get Rid of Resentments

Why do you get angry and annoyed after an argument? A person's normal response would be a long list giving the details as to why the other person was at fault and how unreasonable and illogical, they behaved. You might even say something like this: "I have the right to be mad at my husband speak to me like this."

If you would like to have a life of peace, you need to reverse that kind of thinking. Resentments don't come from the other party's conduct in a fight. They thrive and survive because you aren't willing to end the fight by offering forgiveness, love, and kindness. To quote Lao-Tzu: "Someone must risk returning injury with kindness, or hostility will never turn to goodwill." After all the screaming, yelling and threats have been expressed, it is now time to become calm. No storm will last forever. Hidden inside you are seeds of tranquility. "There is a time for war and a time for peace."

## Step 9: Be Kind, Not Right

To quote an old Chinese proverb: "If you are going to pursue revenge, you have better dig two graves." This says to me that your resentments are going to destroy you. The world is the way it is. People who behave badly are doing exactly what they are supposed to be doing. You have the ability to process it any way you want. If you are angry about all the problems, you are just another person that contributes to the anger pollution. There isn't any reason you should make others wrong just to retaliate if you are done wrong.

Think about someone saying something offensive to you. Instead of heading to resentment, you can depersonalize what you heard and respond instead with kindness. You are freely sending the higher energies of kindness, forgiveness, joy, peace, and love to what comes your way. You do this in order to help yourself. You want to be kind instead of right.

## Step 10: Practice Giving

In the middles of a disagreement or argument, try to give instead of taking before you leave. This means you have to leave your ego behind. Even though it wants to win and show that it is superior by being disrespectful and contrary, your nature would like for you to live in harmony and be at peace. You will be amazed that your quarreling time has gone to zero if you can practice this procedure.

It doesn't matter where you are if you feel a strong emotion well up inside you and you realize you want to "be right" repeat the following words: "Where there is injury, let me bring pardon." Try to give forgiveness. Bring pardon to injury, light to darkness, love to hate. Remember these words and say them daily and they can help you overcome the ego's demands and you will know life at its fullest.

## Step 11: Stop Trying to Be Offended

If you live below or at ordinary levels of awareness, you will spend a lot of energy and time trying to find ways to be offended. Black clouds, someone sneezes, somebody cursed, a stranger was rude, an upsetting news report anything will be fine if you are looking to become offended. Be a person who won't get offended by anything, anyone, or any circumstance. If you have faith in your beliefs, you will see that it is impossible to get offended by the conduct and beliefs of other people.

When you can control getting offended, you are saying that you have control over how you feel, and you have chosen to feel peace no matter what you observe. When you get offended, you will be practicing judgment. You are judging others to be foolish, inconsiderate, arrogant, rude, insensitive, and stupid, and then you see yourself being offended and upset by their actions. What you aren't realizing is that when judging others, you aren't defining them. You are defining yourself as somebody that needs to be the judge of others.

### Step 12: Live in The Present
If you find it hard to forgive, it is usually because you don't live in the present. We say the past is more important. We give most of our attention and energy mourning the past that is forever gone as why we can't be happy now. Doing this assigns responsibility to the past as to why you can't be happy now.

Other creatures don't waste time or thoughts on the future or past. A dog is only a dog. He does a dog at the moment. He doesn't take time thinking about his siblings getting more attention or he doesn't know who his father is. He lives in the now. We have a lot to learn from nature about enjoying the present instead of worrying about the future or being upset about the past. Try to live in the moment by loving the beautifulness around you.

### Step 13: Embrace the Dark Times

In an intelligent universal system that is being supported by Divine Force, there are simply no accidents. Even though it is hard to acknowledge, what happened today, had to happen to get you where you are. Every advance you make spiritually will be preceded by some sort of disaster or fall. During these dark times, broken dreams, abuses, illnesses, times of impoverishment, breakups, tough episodes, and accidents were all supposed to happen. They did happen, so you say they had to and you can't undo them. Embrace, understand, accept, honor and transform them.

### Step 14: Don't Judge

Once you can stop judging and just observe, you will find inner peace. With inner peace, you will be happier and free from all the negative energy. You will find that others are attracted to you because a peaceful person will attract peaceful energy. If I am supposed to be a being of love, this means that I have love inside me and that is all I have to give to others. If somebody chooses to be something that your ego doesn't want, you have to send them ingredients of your higher self which is your Divine Creator and they are love.

Condemnation and criticism of behaviors, feelings, and thoughts of others are a step closer to God realization. It is this consciousness that lets my wishes get fulfilled if they are aligned with your Source of being. Anyone can come up with a huge list of reasons and to why they should be condemnatory and judgmental of others and why you are right. But if you want to perfect your own world, then you have to substitute love for judgments.

### Step 15: Send Love

Patanjali reminds us many thousands of years ago that if we can be steadfast then every living creature won't hostility in our presence. Being steadfast means that we won't slip in abstaining from harming other people.

We are all human. This means we will slip up and retreat from our highest self. We will condemn, criticize, and judge, but this isn't rational for trying to practice sending love. Once you finally realize that when you only send love to others who you have bee criticizing and judging, you will immediately have inner contentment.

You really need to send love in place of criticisms and judgments to others when they hurt your happiness and joy. Hold them in love. When you remain steadfast, when you look at things differently, what you look at will change.

## A Meditation

Visualize yourself at the end of a dispute or fight. Instead of reacting with hurt, revenge, and residual anger, see offerings forgiveness, love, and kindness. Do this instead. Send out "true virtue" thoughts to all resentment that you are currently carrying. Respond by saying this to any altercations: "I end on love, no matter what!"

# Chapter 13:
# EQ Trick #9: Make Others Feel Good Around You

If you have a social anxiety or are shy, it can be hard to make people feel comfortable around you. Your social friends can walk into any room and just light it up. They can instantly make anyone around them feel at ease. What about you? You are the queen of every downhill conversation and all the awkward jokes. This might be an adorable trait with the right people, but it isn't a winning quality when you are trying to make new friends. Don't worry, there are things that you can do to make you more socially graceful and become a person that everybody wants to be around.

The first place to begin is to look at the way you carry yourself. The right body language and facial expressions are quick ways to see who is receptive to your awkwardness. Everyone wants to be comforted and loved and we will approach anyone with an open posture and smiling face. Whereas people who are standing with their arms crossed and a scowl on their face will cause send people packing. If you take anything from this let it be that your body language is key. Here are some other tips to help you give off an approachable vibe to any room.

## Smile

If you warn to make people feel comfortable while showing them you are approachable, what your face is doing is the key. A smile is the best invitation you can send to show you are ready for anything. Make sure it is a natural smile and not plastered on. If it is plastered on, it will seem creepier than inviting.

## Confident Vibes

If you are feeling a bit nervous, giving off a confident vibe will put other people at ease. Being around a confident person is easier than someone who isn't comfortable in their own skin. Be a person who has self-confidence and direction.

## Give Compliments

There are people who have a wonderful ability to give compliments during a conversation. This trait is very likable. Giving compliments while smiling is a great icebreaker. Take this tip and begin applying it to your everyday life. You will soon see a big difference in the way people around you are acting.

## Slow Down When Talking

If you start talking faster when you get excited, you might have to check yourself often. Rapid instructions, questions, talking fast, and constant hand gestures can overwhelm or rattle people near you. If you want people to like being near you, try to slow yourself down.

## Open Body Language

There is a big difference in the way people feel around others who have open body language as opposed to those who are closed off. People that have body language that is open will look relaxed, turn to the person they are talking to, and make eye contact. Try this at your next party and see what happens.

## Show Them You Are Listening

There isn't anything worse than talking to someone and they can't do anything but glance at their phone. If you are guilty of this even if it is accidental, you really need to stop. The person who is talking to you should think they are important to you. Smile if appropriate, make eye contact, and not to let them know you are listening to them.

## Mirror Them

Mirroring people is a sneaky way to make people feel comfortable around you. It begins by your looking at their posture and then let your body do what theirs is. If they sit, you sit. If they stand, you stand. All of a sudden, they are going to feel comfortable without knowing why.

### Create A Homey Atmosphere

Are you having some guests over? The main thing not to do is getting in your head. Remember to be a good hostess. Tell them to relax, sit, get comfortable, and make themselves at home. Bring them drinks, coffee, tea, snacks, anything to give off positive vibes. If you are feeling comfortable, they will feel comfortable.

### Be Hilarious

Every person in the world who is warm and welcoming will have one thing in common. They all have a great sense of humor. If you realize you are stiffening up or you don't know what to say. Telling a joke is a great place to start. It shows them that you are happy, and it will draw them toward you. If you joke around, everybody else will too.

### Be Honest

People have an innate ability to know when others aren't being truthful or if they are holding back. It isn't a good comfort level. This is why being honest is a good idea. If you can tell the truth, you will be able to build a better, more meaningful relationship. That's your goal, right?

## Be Nice

Above all else, be nice. The best thing you can do to make people feel comfortable is the kind and gracious to everybody. We shouldn't have to tell you but doing small things, sending sweet notes, or saying thank you goes a long way when making people feel at ease. That is the cornerstone to helping people feel comfortable around you. Give compliments, be kind, be nice, and you will be making new friends quickly.

# Chapter 14:
# EQ Trick #10: Manage Anger

Do you get mad when you get cut off in traffic? When your child won't cooperate, does it cause your blood pressure to boil? Anger can be a healthy emotion and it is completely normal. You have to learn to deal with it in positive ways. Anger that isn't under control can take a toll on your relationship and health. The main goal in controlling anger is to reduce both the physiological arousal and the emotional feelings that caused the anger. There isn't any way to avoid or get rid of the people or things that make you angry and you can't change them. There are ways to control your reaction.

### Could You Be Too Angry?

There are tests that can measure how intense your feelings are, how prone you are to anger, and if you can handle it. If you have a problem with anger, you probably already know it. If you see yourself acting in ways that seen frightening or out of control, you need to figure out ways that can help you deal with this emotion.

## Why Are Some Angrier Than Others?

Some people are just naturally more "hotheaded" than others. They will get angrier easier and more intensely than the average person. There are also people who won't show their anger in loud ways but are constantly grumpy and irritable. People who are easily angered don't throw things and curse; they sometimes will withdraw, get physically ill, or sulk.

People that get angry easily will have what psychologists call "low tolerance for frustration". This means that they feel like they shouldn't be subjected to annoyance, inconvenience, or frustration. They aren't able to take things in stride, and they get infuriated with a situation that seems unjust like being corrected for pronouncing a word wrong.

What causes these people to act this way? There are many things that can cause it. One could be physiological or genetic: Some evidence has shown that children can be born easily angered, touchy, and irritable. These signs are apparent from an early age. Another one could be sociocultural. This means anger is thought to be negative. We have been taught that it is fine to express depression, anxiety, and other emotions but not anger. Because of this, we haven't learned how to channel or handle it the right way. Research has also shown that a family's background can play a role, too. People who get angry easily come from families that are chaotic, disruptive and weren't skilled in emotional communications. If are ready to get control of your anger, here are ten anger management tips for you.

### Step 1: Always Think Before Speaking
During the high point of a conflict, it is easy to say things that you might regret later. Take some time to collect your thoughts before you say anything. If others are involved, this time will let them cool off, too.

### Step 2: Express Your Anger, After You Have Calmed Down
Once you are able to think clearly, let others know your feelings of frustration in a nonconfrontational but assertive way. Voice your needs and concerns directly and clearly without trying to hurt or control others.

### Step 3: Exercise
Working out could help reduce the stress that has caused you to get angry. If you feel that your anger is getting worse, go for a run or walk. Find an activity that you enjoy doing.

### Step 4: Get Some Alone Time
Children aren't the only ones who deserve a timeout. Take breaks during the day when you start to feel stressed. Taking some quiet time

could help you get prepared for the rest of your day without getting angry.

## Step 5: Find Solutions

Stop focusing on the thing that made you mad. Try to resolve the problem. Is it your child's messy room that's irritating you? Just close their door. Does your significant other always come home late for supper? Try cooling supper later or just eat alone. Just remember that anger isn't going to fix anything. It might just make things worse.

## Step 6: Try Using "I" Statements

If you place blame or criticize, this might increase tension. Try using "I" statements when describing the problem. Be specific and respectful. Instead of saying "you never help out around the house," say "it upsets me when you leave the table without offering to help."

## Step 7: Never Hold Grudges

Forgiveness is a great tool. If you let negative feelings and anger crowd out your positive feelings, you might get swallowed by your sense of injustice and bitterness. If you can learn to forgive people who have angered you, both of you could learn from this situation and you might even make your relationship stronger.

## Step 8: Release Tension with Humor

Being silly might diffuse tension. You can use humor the help you with what is making you angry. This might get rid of all the unrealistic expectations you have for the ways you think things need to go. Stay away from sarcasm as it can make things worse by hurting other's feelings.

## Step 9: Learn How to Relax

Use skills to help you relax when you get angry. Try repeating a calming phrase or word, imagine a scene that relaxes you, or do some deep breathing. You could also listen to music, do yoga, or write your thoughts down in a journal. Whatever you can do to relax will help diffuse the situation.

## Step 10: Understand When You Need Help

It is challenging when you are learning to control your anger. It is okay to seek help if your anger seems out of control and causes you to hurt others or do things you regret.

# Chapter 15: FAQ

You have been given a lot of information about emotional intelligence, but you might still have some questions. Here is a list of the most frequently asked questions about emotional intelligence.

### Emotional Intelligence, What Is It?

This is an ability to be able to identify your emotions. Being able to know how these emotions impact you and the ability to manage them. Emotional intelligence also includes the ability to understand other people's emotions, understand how these emotions impact your relationship and are able to self-correct. EQ and IQ are not the same things. IQ is your capacity for intelligence. IQ measures cognitive abilities. This includes the ability to use reasoning, logic, memorize, perceive, and analyze correctly.

### Why Is Emotional Intelligence Important?

This is the key to your happiness. It helps you become a content person that relates well to other people. It is the foundation for managing relationships, social awareness, and self-management. Emotions that cause distress and aren't well managed can affect your ability to get your work done, focus, and think.

Conflicts with other people can't be resolved successfully if you can't address the emotions that caused the conflict and any pain that came with it.

### Can A Person Improve Their Emotional Intelligence?

Emotional Intelligence is different the Intellectual Capacity. IQ is fixed and can't be changed. Emotional Intelligence can be developed with time. Anyone can improve their emotional intelligence.

### What Skills Are Needed to Improve Emotional Intelligence?

There are five skills that can help raise Emotional Intelligence:

- Ability to resolve conflicts in a positive way.

- Use humor to cope with challenges.

- Improve communicating nonverbally.

- Improve emotional awareness.

- Reduces stress quickly.

**Emotional Intelligence Versus Regular Intelligence**
Basically, Emotional Intelligence is:

- Knowing that actions are determined by feelings and emotions and by beliefs and thoughts.

- Knowing how it works.

- Knowing this applies to everybody.

- Acting the right way.

**When Looking for A Job, Why Isn't Technical Skill Enough?**
Everyone has Emotional Intelligence. It is essential in business. Here lately it's been described and identified as another aspect of a person's mind. This is useful since it helps people get better. Persons purchase things from others. A person works with others. Being able to relate to others is essential in business. People that ignore this aspect of work will have problems and won't be able to understand why they are having problems or how to fix these problems. Emotional Intelligence can help

people know why what they are doing works and help them to improve consciously.

### Can A Person's Emotional Intelligence Be Tested?

You can find tools that say they can measure Emotional Intelligence. It has not been determined completely if they provide anything that is useful. There isn't anything positive that says it can measure Emotional Intelligence. This question is an open one. A person who wants to measure their emotional intelligence isn't very emotionally intelligent.

### When Talking About Business Why Are There Emotions Involved?

Beliefs and emotions drive emotions. If you are in a manager's position and you need an employee to change their behavior, you will be more successful if you can involve their beliefs and emotions. If you own a business and want others to purchase your services and products, you will be more successful if you can involve people's emotions. People make decisions based on their emotions.

### Is Sentimentality Being Favored Over Logic?

When talking about sentimentality, you are referring to something so overly sentimental it is sickening, then no. If you are talking about being "concerned with the sentiment" such as emotions, then it could increase a person's awareness of Emotional Intelligence. If you are asking if within our logic based and rational culture our emotions will ever dominate logic, I would have to say no.

## Is Emotional Intelligence A Form of Manipulation?

Everything can be manipulated in one way or another. Paying a person, a ridiculous salary is a form of manipulation. Having to write an essay in red instead of blue, is manipulation. The main thing to know is the intention behind the behavior. Emotional Intelligence is just one of a lot of things that people can use to manipulate others. It isn't manipulation itself.

## What Characteristics Will People Have with High Emotional Intelligence?

People who have high Emotional Intelligence will have a better sense of self-awareness that leads to success. They will understand and be more empathic of others. They work better with others. Having Emotional Intelligence is needed to be a leader.

## Can I Improve Emotional Intelligence?

If you want to improve your Emotional Intelligence, you should develop and practice self-awareness. Don't judge others. Stop trying to always be right.

## Can Emotional Intelligence Get Better Results on A Professional Exam?

Most formal exams are restricted to a person's self-awareness. You should be able to handle stress. Whatever state you need to be in such as positive, motivated, or staying calm, you need to work on it to enhance that ability. Having high Emotional Intelligence means you are a good communicator. What you write could be influenced by your communication skills.

## Should Accountants Worry About Emotional Intelligence?

Being an accountant is an occupation where emotions can be excluded. Accountants are people who work for others and with others. A successful accountant can work successfully with other people. You should try to increase your Emotional Intelligence to help with clients.

## Conclusion

You have learned quite a bit about emotional intelligence and its importance. Now it is in your hand to work on your emotional intelligence. It's important that, if you have struggled with EQ in that past, you take active steps now to improve your EQ now. Emotional intelligence plays an important part in our lives and how we interact with people everybody.

If you find this book helpful in anyway a review to support my endeavors is much appreciated.

**Emotional Intelligence Mastery**

Stephen Patterson

www.ingramcontent.com/pod-product-compliance
Lightning Source LLC
Chambersburg PA
CBHW060451080526
44584CB00015B/1405